THE DRUM IS A WILD WOMAN

THE DRUM IS A WILD WOMAN

Jazz and Gender in African Diaspora Literature

Patricia G. Lespinasse

University Press of Mississippi / Jackson

The University Press of Mississippi is the scholarly publishing agency of the Mississippi Institutions of Higher Learning: Alcorn State University, Delta State University, Jackson State University, Mississippi State University, Mississippi University for Women, Mississippi Valley State University, University of Mississippi, and University of Southern Mississippi.

www.upress.state.ms.us

The University Press of Mississippi is a member of the Association of University Presses.

First printing 2022

∞

Library of Congress Cataloging-in-Publication Data

Names: Lespinasse, Patricia G., author.
Title: The drum is a wild woman : jazz and gender in African diaspora literature / Patricia G. Lespinasse.
Description: Jackson : University Press of Mississippi, 2022. | Includes bibliographical references and index.
Identifiers: LCCN 2021041770 (print) | LCCN 2021041771 (ebook) | ISBN 9781496836038 (hardback) | ISBN 9781496836021 (trade paperback) | ISBN 9781496836045 (epub) | ISBN 9781496836052 (epub) | ISBN 9781496836069 (pdf) | ISBN 9781496836076 (pdf)
Subjects: LCSH: Jazz in literature. | Jazz—History and criticism. | Women in music | African American women authors. | Music and literature. | Wild women in literature. | BISAC: LITERARY CRITICISM / Feminist | MUSIC / Genres & Styles / Jazz
Classification: LCC ML3506 .L46 2022 (print) | LCC ML3506 (ebook) | DDC 781.6509—dc23
LC record available at https://lccn.loc.gov/2021041770
LC ebook record available at https://lccn.loc.gov/2021041771

British Library Cataloging-in-Publication Data available

Note to readers: In this book, some quoted material contains racial slurs directed toward Black people. While those words have been retained, this is in no way an endorsement of the use of such slurs outside a scholarly context.

CONTENTS

ACKNOWLEDGMENTS

I would first and foremost like to acknowledge and thank Jehovah for blessing me with the peace of mind to write. I also must thank my parents, who instilled in me a love for literature and Haitian culture. Throughout this process they showered me with encouragement and motivated me by always asking: "kilè liv la ap soti?"

Growing up, my parents would host a celebration for my siblings and me every time one of us graduated. The parties consisted of our large family and the same friends from our tight-knit Haitian community, with a sprinkling of outsiders. My father called them our "village." I imagine that after the first few parties everyone knew the protocol: before the festivities would officially begin there had to be a prayer, and right before the prayer there was "the speech." My dad, the grand orator, would begin by thanking the "village" for their love and support and my mom (the grand editor of his speeches) would stand right by his side making sure he got it right. Indeed, it took a village to raise us and a village to complete this book project. In the course of writing this book I have relied on readers, colleagues, scholars, friends, family, and editors. Although it is impossible to name all who contributed to this project, I still appreciate everyone in my village even if they are not named here.

There were a few people who had an important influence in my life: Beverly Fields, the director of the McNair Scholars program at St. John's University, who first encouraged me to be a scholar. I am also grateful to Derek Owens, who introduced me to the field of English and served as a model scholar. A special thank you to Carlyle Thompson and Sue Houchins for their time and dedication in my formative years.

At Columbia University I was fortunate to work with three brilliant scholars on various projects: Farah J. Griffin, Robert G. O'Meally, and the late Manning Marable. I will be forever grateful to them for their teaching, advising, and encouraging my passion for African American literature and culture.

I would also like to extend my deep appreciation to those who directly aided in the publication of this book. Such luminaries as Farah J. Griffin, Robert G. O'Meally, and the late Marcellus Blount supported and guided this project from its inception. Your detailed comments allowed me to think beyond the text and push my analysis to the limits. I am grateful to Imani Perry, Herman Beavers, and John Szwed for inspiring and assisting me at the crucial early stages of my work. A fellowship in African and African Diaspora Literature from Rutgers University afforded me the opportunity to work with the late Cheryl A. Wall, who gave me the time and resources to research and revise the book.

The Drum Is a Wild Woman was immeasurably improved by the insightful comments of those who read it in chapter or manuscript form. I would like to greatly acknowledge Joanne V. Gabbin, Nkiru Nzegwu, Kelly Baker Josephs, Michelle Stephens, Evie Shockley, Michael O. West, and Anne C. Bailey for their insight, suggestions, and support.

Special appreciation goes to Diedra Harris Kelley and the Romare Bearden Foundation for permission to use Romare Bearden's *Showtime* as the book cover. I also greatly appreciate the editorial and production staff at the University Press of Mississippi. Thank you to my editors: Vijay Shah for his insightful suggestions and for making a home for this book, and Lisa McMurtray for her patient and steadfast commitment to its publication. I also thank the staff and expert readers from the University Press of Mississippi for their critiques and suggestions.

Finally, I'd also like to thank my siblings, Patrick and Pascale, for their unconditional love and support: Patrick for asking the difficult intellectual questions and providing edits that ultimately improved my writing; and Pascale for providing the emotional support that has carried me through to the end of the book project. Last but not least, my village would not be complete without my beautiful girls, Chloe and Camryn. Thank you for all that you do to keep me grounded and steeped in joy, laughter, and love . . . mommy writes for you.

THE DRUM IS A WILD WOMAN

A NEW BEAT, GENERATIONS LATER

Modern Jazz and African Diaspora Women's Writing

In 1956 Duke Ellington discussed the title of his album, *A Drum Is a Woman*: "You know how it is," said Duke Ellington, "a musician will say to his woman—'Here's $2 baby, go on down to the tavern or the movies and leave me alone for a while with the drum.' And so we say a drum is a woman—it kind of takes the place of her."[1] Duke Ellington's words reveal a telling perception about the role of women in jazz discourse—jilted by the male musician and replaced by the drum.

Ellington's album cover further illustrates this personification of the drum as a woman. The cover features an image of a woman's body obscured by a drum. This objectification of women lends itself to a critical reading of the role of women in Ellington's album and modern jazz music in general. If the drum can take the place of a woman, then what is the relationship between Black women, the drum, and modern jazz music?

Overall accounts of jazz's early development in the early nineteenth century have involved women and drums well before the music was deemed jazz. Ted Gioia's *The History of Jazz* begins with the observations of Benjamin Henry Latrobe in 1819. Latrobe observed a drumming ritual in Congo Square and described the participants engaging in a ritualized drumming session:

> An elderly black man sits astride a large cylindrical drum. Using his fingers and the edge of his hand, he jabs repeatedly at the drumhead—which is around a foot in diameter and probably made from an animal skin—evoking a throbbing pulsation with rapid, sharp strokes. A second drummer, holding his instrument between his knees, joins in, playing with the same

staccato attack. A third black man, seated on the ground, plucks at a string instrument, the body of which is roughly fashioned from a calabash. Another calabash has been made into a drum, and a woman beats at it with two short sticks. One voice, then other voices join in. A dance of seeming contradictions accompanies this musical give-and-take, a moving hieroglyph that appears, on the one hand, informal and spontaneous yet, on closer inspection, ritualized and precise. It is a dance of massive proportions. (Gioia 3)

In Latrobe's account, the drum is central and far outnumbers other instruments, thereby making it the instrumental focus of the scene. Interestingly, the drum seemed always in relation to its player whether the player sat astride it, held it between his knees, or beat on it. In addition, women were playing alongside the men. Women were not marginalized in this space, but rather contributed to the musical landscape in a significant way. Further, Latrobe noted that upon hearing the music, a crowd of bodies came forward and formed groups to dance as the women chanted: "a dense crowd of dark bodies forms into circular groups—perhaps five or six hundred individuals moving in time to the pulsations of the music, some swaying gently, others aggressively stomping their feet. A number of women in the group begin chanting" (Latrobe 1). Similar scenes in Congo Square reiterated the confluence of the drums, women, and dancing within the square. Thus it was not by chance that when Duke Ellington set out to compose an allegory of the birth of jazz music, he chose both the drum and a woman as central symbols of the music and Congo Square as the setting. Therefore, by likening a drum to a woman on his album, Ellington posited the female body as central to jazz's origins.

The Drum Is a Wild Woman explores the complex relationship between Black women and modern jazz after World War II. The book title is taken from Duke Ellington's 1956 *A Drum Is a Woman*, also known as the "mother of all albums." The album-turned-television-show delineates a musical allegory about the origins of jazz. The discourse surrounding the music's birth centers on the blues. Whether it be southern blues, drenched in the fields of oppressive plantations, or northern blues, obscured in the dim lights of a crowded city, jazz's flourishing would not be possible without the blues or women. From women's foundational classic blues recordings in the 1920s to their instrumental role as musicians and mentors to a generation of jazz artists, the contributions of Black women seem just as fundamental to jazz discourse as a drum is to any jazz composition.

However, Duke Ellington's album seemingly told a different story. From the album cover to the lyrics, *A Drum* also suggested that a woman's body, rather than her musical contributions, takes center stage. More specifically, the album's cover and the typecast role that women play in the television program of *A Drum Is a Woman* indicate that women are actually mired in a complex history of jazz discourse as both subject and object.

The central image on *A Drum is a Woman*'s album cover is the female body. The cover renders the gendered body faceless and irrelevant as she sits with her back to the audience. The sexualized posture of her hands is outstretched in ecstasy or worship and her buttocks cupped by the drum. In this pose, the female body becomes immobilized as her legs are molded into the drum image and invisible. The red dress that she wears is a signifier for both passion and death. Her blonde hair and skin tone would suggest her race; however, in this period album covers commonly used white women to sell more records. Yet, a Black woman plays the principal role of Madam Zajj in the television series derived from the album, on CBS's *US Steel Hour*. Madam Zajj plays the role of intermediary as she guides Carribee Joe through the history of jazz.

In Ellington's musical allegory, the African enchantress Madam Zajj cries, "I am not a Drum but a Woman." She subsequently refuses to settle for confinement in the jungle with Carribee Joe, instead setting off on her own to find other "Joes" that satisfy her need for a musical partner. Critics have interpreted Madam Zajj as a metaphor for jazz and described her travels as conveying Ellington's historical views regarding jazz's origins.

However, Madam Zajj's actions as seen in the television series have not yet been examined through a feminist lens. Throughout the musical allegory, Ellington's narrative leads listeners through the worlds in which Madam Zajj seeks to subvert the politics of respectability for women after World War II. Defined by historian Evelyn Brooks

Higginbotham as a politics intended to describe morally responsible work done by upper-middle-class Black women at the turn of the twentieth century, the politics of respectability transformed into a way of policing Black women's bodies (sexually, politically, and socially) and imposing a Victorian sense of respectability and accountability.[2]

Madam Zajj discards the politics of respectability and decides to improvise a new life for herself beyond Carribee Joe's beloved jungle. We follow her rhythm from the Caribbean to New Orleans to New York and finally to the moon and back. Perhaps unintentionally, Ellington delivered not only a feminist narrative about women's complex relationship to jazz, as presented in the album cover, but also a platform that enables Madam Zajj to be inscribed as a Wild Woman. The Wild Woman, a term that describes the female vocalist in the classic blues tradition, used music—specifically, blues and jazz—to push the boundaries of Black womanhood outside the confines of respectability. This study borrows the term from the classic blues tradition and extends its reach into jazz discourse. In texts that refer to jazz in form or content, the Wild Woman is a figure of resistance who uses language, image, and improvisation to refashion herself from object to subject. Viewed through a feminist lens, Madam Zajj appears not only as a woman but also as one of the first examples of a Wild Woman at the center of jazz rather than on its periphery.

This book begins to define a counter-tradition within women's writing that involves the reinvention and reclamation of a modern jazz discourse with women at the center. Despite their alienation from bebop, women in other contexts have found jazz music empowering and have demonstrated this power through language. This study thus explores the complex relationship between women and modern jazz music in contemporary African diasporic literature.

In 1988 Jayne Cortez responded to A Drum's sexist portrayal of women in her poem "If A Drum Is a Woman," questioning the inequities within the allegory. Her revisionist poetry provided a literary response not only to Ellington but also to the silencing of women within the jazz tradition. In "If the Drum Is a Woman," Cortez addresses Duke Ellington's allegory by presenting the reality of the analogy that compares a drum to a woman.

Cortez employs rhetorical questions throughout the poem to confront the idea that comparing the drum to a woman entails understanding the violence that comes not only with the analogy but also with the forceful neglect of women beyond the jazz tradition. Cortez's rhetorical questions transitioned into a rhetorical analysis of how drums in Ellington's allegory are to be upheld and revered. However, in the reality of the African American female experience, if the drum is a woman she must endure violence and is in constant danger of physical abuse. Cortez confronts the idea of the instrument as a woman and describes how one might consider the various realities of being a woman. This monograph answers both of these calls by asserting that, as women began to rewrite these narratives about the relationship of women and jazz in the 1970s and 1980s, they decidedly constructed the woman as a "Wild Woman."

Jazz has remained a source of inspiration for writers throughout its development. Since the 1912 publication of James Weldon Johnson's *Autobiography of an Ex-Colored Man*, the music has influenced the subject, style, and form of twentieth-century American literature and culture. Jazz's cultural influence also recurs in the writings of authors, such as Jack Kerouac, Ralph Ellison, Langston Hughes, and Amiri Baraka, among others, who have been regarded as writers of jazz literature—writing that infuses jazz's syncopated rhythms and cultural ideology into narratives that portray existential quandaries, social resistance, and the fight for freedom. Yet aside from Sherrie Tucker's and Farah Jasmine Griffin's research, the influence of jazz music on Black women's fiction has not received the critical attention it deserves.[3]

Jurgen Grandt approaches the topic of Black women's fiction and jazz music but concentrates on a jazz aesthetic rather than a gendered analysis. Although Grandt includes Toni Morrison and touches on gender politics through Ann Petry's *The Street*, he does not interrogate the ways in which Black women's jazz fiction reconstructs the role of Black women in jazz discourse. However, this study emphasizes how African American women writers create dissonant sounds that echo the Beat Generation's motives and broaden our understanding of jazz literary discourse.

Women writers from the African diaspora have challenged and revised major tropes and concerns of jazz literary discourse since the bebop era (mid-1940s). By underscoring the extent to which gender is already embedded in jazz discourse, this book responds to and corrects studies and narratives that tell the story of jazz through a male-centered lens. The book concentrates on women writers but avoids silencing their male contemporaries, instead examining the many ways that the female narratives respond to male-centered jazz texts.

This study emphasizes three recurring literary motifs—cry-and-response, the Wild Woman, and the improvised moment—in jazz novels, short stories, and poetry published since 1946, comparing works by Ann Petry, Gayl Jones, Toni Morrison, Edwidge Danticat, Paule Marshall, and Maya Angelou with pieces by Albert Murray, Ralph Ellison, James Baldwin, Richard Wright, and Amiri Baraka. This comparative focus on gendered readings of jazz literature contests the emphasis on the male-centered narrative, presenting a counternarrative about the significance of improvisation as a tool for resistance across gendered boundaries. By foregrounding the vexed negotiations around gender and jazz discourse, this book tells an empowering story about the formation of Black female subjectivity and intercultural identity.

Sherrie Tucker initiated this approach in her trailblazing essay, "Where the Blues and the Truth Lay Hiding: Rememory of Jazz in Black Women's Fiction."[4] Tucker's essay stands as one of the first to focus exclusively on Black women's fiction and its significant role in the discourse of jazz studies. Tucker writes that Black women's fiction is a space where one can find a "record of meaning, as well as existence, for Black women in the field of jazz." She elaborates that Black women's fiction is a "site in which Black women have long written with authority" (26). Yet, as Farah Griffin notes, the canon of jazz literature is devoid of Black women's fiction.[5] Aside from Toni Morrison's *Jazz* and Gayl Jones's *Corregidora*, which have appeared "on syllabi, as symposia topics, or in a myriad of recent anthologies devoted to jazz literature" (Griffin, "It Takes" 349), works by Black women writers have yet to gain the status of jazz fiction.

Griffin's essay, published in *Big Ears: Listening for Gender in Jazz Studies* (2008), the first anthology to focus on gender and jazz studies, significantly extends Tucker's assertions by contending Black women's fiction, specifically Toni Cade Bambara's "Medley" and Sherley Ann Williams's "Tell Martha Not to Moan," as significant works of jazz literature. Griffin defines jazz literature as "poems, novels, short stories, and literary essays that reference the music and musicians as central to the work's form or content" ("It Takes" 349). Her essay draws our attention to how both Bambara and Williams create texts that "respond to discourses surrounding the music, be they other forms of fiction or stories and stereotypes that abound within the jazz community" (350). Griffin's essay significantly calls for a jazz literature canon inclusive of the jazz fiction created by Black women. Griffin makes it possible to establish a canon of Black women's jazz literature and to take seriously how their fiction is informed by the music and the music by their lived experience. Griffin's and Tucker's articles lay the foundation for the kinds of interventions that this study seeks to make within jazz discourse and African American women's social history.

The absence of extensive scholarship on the subject of jazz in Black women's fiction might result from the fact that Black women writers create jazz texts that are difficult to analyze. Like Griffin and Tucker, I regard Black women's jazz literature as a site that can describe the points in which Black women entered the history of music; yet unlike them, I provide a theory for reading the relationship between jazz music and women in jazz texts.

Feminist jazz texts offer narratives about how the music influenced the daily lives of women and served as a catalyst for their acts of resistance. The narratives I discuss here qualify as feminist jazz texts not only because they are informed by the music but also because they construct new possibilities for understanding the music and, more broadly, African American life after World War II. Black women writers adopt jazz and its ideology as a psychological catalyst for their protagonists' acts of resistance. As Baraka notes, the psychological catalyst provides extensive information about the music, making "the music the exact registration of the social and cultural thinking of a whole generation of black Americans" (*Black Music* 20). Thus these authors endeavor to create what scholar Robert O'Meally describes as a jazz-literary correspondence by means of the people.[6] Black women authors not only speak with authority about jazz, but appropriate jazz's fundamental component, improvisation, throughout their jazz texts.

I define the feminist jazz text as incorporating three recurring motifs: cry-and-response, the Wild Woman, and the moment of improvisation. Unlike Tucker, who analyzes the role of the female musician, and Griffin, who explores the role of the women who share their lives with musicians, I take interest in the ways in which Black women writers create texts that incorporate components of jazz music. Specifically, I explore how female jazz characters become the cultural and social artifacts of the revolutionary bebop era. Thus, these women authors create jazz-like characters—musicians with a platform, failed musicians devoid of a platform, and regular people influenced by the music who appropriate its components. To this end, jazz serves as a vehicle in which characters can take action and assert themselves to achieve freedom and agency.

African American and Caribbean American women writers reclaim the jazz tradition by extending and revising the gender themes/issues proffered by the classic blues tradition, as marked by a self-reflexive, public meditation on taboo subjects in the lives of African Americans and African American women specifically. Unlike the classic blues tradition, the jazz tradition focused on men and is characterized by improvisation through individual assertion, democratic ideals via group/community dynamics, and the attainment of freedom. Further, the literary texts analyzed in this study move beyond presenting a jazz aesthetic, extending and revising the tradition through narrative innovations that demonstrate the extent to which the influence of jazz in American culture suffuses the works and thereby the culture.

Scholar Hazel Carby remarks that, although the classic blues period ended in 1929, the power of the female classic blues singer was "resurrected in a different moment of black power; reemerging in Gayl Jones *Corregidora*" (20).[7] My study of texts informed by the classic blues tradition includes but is not limited to the assertive female blues singer. The classic blues tradition has been resurrected in the literary contributions of African American women writers. This resurrection not only extends the blues tradition but also revolutionizes it, creating new rhetorical modes within African American discourse, constructing spaces for agency by means of spontaneous action, and focusing on the Wild Woman, a demoralized character who is a product of the historical trauma of slavery and the perpetual effects of racist and sexist ideology.

Oral Tradition: If in jazz music musicians use instruments to "tell the story," the narratives under consideration highlight the language of the oral tradition by showing its limitation as a musical signifier. In the jazz text, the oral tradition becomes the means by which jazz music is championed through such literary conventions as repetition, improvisation, and reconfiguration. The jazz text distinguishes itself from the blues text as it reconfigures call-and-response into a more nuanced cry-and-response dialogue. Cry-and-response is rooted in ritual and is used as a coded language.

Jazz Moment: Borrowing from Ralph Ellison,[8] this book defines the jazz moment as a moment of individual assertion where one's identity is shaped: an improvisational moment where history and memory collide to form a temporal space for agency and subjectivity. According to music critic Albert Murray, the moment happens in the "break." The jazz moment troubles the idealized view of improvisation by depicting the moment of improvisation within the act of retributive violence performed by the soloist or jazz-like character. My book analyzes the image of the soloist/improviser through a feminist lens and demonstrates how the jazz moment is constructed to create an anti-heroic subject. According to Murray, "in order to be a hero one has to slay the dragon." In these revisionist texts, the dragon slayer or soloist/improviser becomes the anti-hero.

Wild Women: The Wild Woman archetype is a figure of resistance. These wild women arm themselves with figurative and literal weapons such as their sexuality, voice, knives, and pestles. These weapons serve to preserve their dignity and allow them to gain agency within the jazz moment of improvisation. What differentiates the wild woman from other women is her determination to reconstruct the characteristics others use to define her to reclaim power over her body.

The interplay between oral tradition, the jazz moment of improvisation, and Wild Women can be seen throughout each chapter as women writers use improvisation, jazz's quintessential element, to expand on and substantially revise the role of Black women in jazz discourse. Each chapter in this book relies on a feminist reading to unearth the three motifs within an interdisciplinary and transnational context.

Chapter 1 explores the way in which Maya Angelou's jazz short story, "Reunion," is structured like an evolving jazz tune, circular in form, highlighting the music of the era and using it as a vehicle to detail the social history of Black female resistance and its relationship to jazz music. Set in the 1940s, Angelou describes a virtuosic Black female piano player, reminiscent of jazz pianist Mary Lou Williams, who channels the essence of bebop in a piano solo that transforms her from object of denigration to subject of improvisation. Angelou explores the bebop era, a particular moment in jazz history bereft of stories pertaining to African American women musicians, to provide a counternarrative that places the Black female musician/improviser as central to jazz discourse. Angelou's short story becomes a site or repository for the cultural memory of African American women and jazz music. Read through a feminist lens, "Reunion" underscores the evolution of the wild woman or female jazz musician from object to subject and the nature of cry-and-response, and highlights the "jazz moment" as a moment of resistance, one that enables African American female musicians to transcend racial and gendered boundaries in order to gain agency and subjectivity through the music.

Chapter 2 focuses on the language of resistance in Gayl Jones's *Corregidora*, analyzing the vocabulary of the jazz text. I analyze the language of the jazz text and its relationship to African American oral tradition. This chapter focuses on moments of "musical signifying," the rhetorical use of musical tropes subsumed under the master trope of call-and-response (calls, cries, hollers), to outline a theory of cry-and-response. Because musical signifying, as noted by Albert Murray, carries with it a "telling effect" that "asserts, alleges, quests, requests, and implies . . . mocks, groans, concurs, and signifies misgivings and suspicions," it is used as a means to subvert language through the incorporation of silences, inarticulacies, and breaks in dialogue. Silences, breaks, and inarticulate utterings signify on the improvisation inherent in the cry-and-response dialogue, as Jones's use of ritualized dialogue is another form of resistance. The novel serves as a critique of African American oral tradition and the limitations of language to "speak" or "bear witness" to the emotional experience of generations of African American women who must bear the legacy of slavery.

Chapter 3 highlights moments of resistance in Morrison's *The Bluest Eye*, using the Trueblood episode in Ellison's *Invisible Man* as a lens to compare and contrast the "jazz moment." The complex issue of incestuous rape, found within that moment, is placed at the forefront of Morrison's novel as a response to, and as a revision of, Ralph Ellison's male-centered Trueblood episode. My contention is that Morrison's novel echoes the Trueblood episode through Cholly and Pecola Breedlove's narrative. Morrison pushes the boundaries of that episode beyond the "blues idiom" and into the realm of what is characterized as the "jazz moment" of resistance. Although many scholars have analyzed the rape-scene in *The Bluest Eye*, I propose a rereading of the scene through a jazz lens and posit the moments leading up to, during, and after the rape as jazz moments. Morrison constructs the jazz moment, within the context of the African American family, as a moment of incestuous violence, drawing attention to internal issues of the African American family and, by extension, the African American community.

Chapter 4 interrogates the literary figures of resistance in Morrison's *Jazz* and Petry's *The Street*. This chapter examines the term "wild woman" as defined by Angela Davis: "The woman who consciously rejects mainstream values, especially those prescribing passivity in relations with men." I explore the literary evolution of the African American wild woman from a sexual object to an improvising subject, beginning in 1852 with Harriet Beecher Stowe's *Uncle Tom's Cabin* to the 1992 publication of Toni Morrison's *Jazz*. I contend that Morrison and Petry endeavor to deconstruct the image of the wild woman by exploring prior layers of meaning and significance attributed to her. *Jazz* depicts wild women who resist established societal definitions on morality and redefine what it means to be wild—without regulation or control. My analysis of the wild woman as an agent of improvisation in Petry's *The Street* explores how the jazz moment of improvisation serves to disrupt notions of African American female identity within the context of intimate violence and male-female power relations.

Chapter 5 analyzes resistance in the Caribbean American jazz narrative. The jazz ethos is depicted as the quintessential marker of freedom and agency for immigrants attempting to assimilate into American culture in Edwidge Danticat's *Breath Eyes Memory*. This chapter begins with an analysis of the presence of jazz through the character portrayal of Joseph in order to demonstrate how jazz music is prevalent throughout the text and is used as the bridge that connects the various diasporic identities in the novel. The Haitian oral tradition of *andaki*, coded language, is akin to the African American tradition of cry-and-response, both exhibiting that through oral traditions a culture may resist the dominant linguistic ideologies and subjects can thereby gain power. Then the chapter moves from analyzing the *andaki* dialect to the unspoken language of Vodou by interrogating the presence of Erzulie throughout the text. Erzulie is constructed as the Wild Woman archetype and serves as idol to the women in the novel through the examples of Martine, Sophie, and Atie who must adopt Erzulie's key characteristics to challenge patriarchal nationalist ideologies that relegate the female body to domestic spaces and re-move agency from the individual woman. Finally, the chapter looks at the role of intimate violence in the novel as one that echoes the trope of incestuous rape found in African American texts and demonstrate how Danticat complicates the incest taboo by figuring women as the main victimizers of the female body. It concludes with a discussion on the relationship among jazz, resistance, and sexual violence in the Caribbean American novel.

Chapter 6 further expounds on the significance of jazz and gender within the Caribbean American novel. This chapter focuses on Paule Marshall's *The Fisher King* and proposes a matrilineal reading of the women who populate the narrative and serve as the archival bodies that "pass on" the legacy of jazz and ultimately free the music from its structural bondage through language and image. In this chapter I contend that Marshall creates a space (literally and figuratively) for Black female agency and challenge male-dominated narratives about jazz music in America and abroad. Marshall constructs varied im-ages of Black women as improvisers/innovators/creators in order to place women at the center of jazz literary discourse. Ultimately, *The Fisher King* becomes a prime example of Marshall's uncanny ability to (re)inscribe the interconnections between Black women, jazz music, and African diaspora literature.

The conclusion reiterates the central claims in *The Drum Is a Wild Woman* and examines the literary politics and poetics found in jazz poetry and dance. The chapter returns to Duke Ellington's musical allegory, *A Drum Is a Woman*, as a critical lens to analyze Jayne Cortez's revisionist poetry and Carmen De Lavallade's jazz choreography. Similar to previous chapters, the musical allegory contains the three tropes and can be viewed as the "call" to which Cortez and De Lavallade "respond." By exploring the presence of these tropes in other genres, I extend the jazz lens and establish an interdisciplinary and transnational approach for reading gender in jazz discourse.

My conceptual orientation throughout the book is to center contemporary African diaspora women writers whose texts foreground the three tropes (wild women, cry-and-response, and the jazz moment) that connect Black women's writings to jazz music. Therefore, I end by indicating the usefulness of a womanist jazz lens, while pointing to other narratives and texts that engage these tropes in similar reconstructive projects.

The jazz texts discussed here use improvisation to empower marginalized characters as they negotiate racism, sexual oppression, and intimate violence. Although these novels refer to jazz to different degrees, improvisation plays a role in the evolution of a marginalized Wild Woman character who must go from object of the gaze to subject of her own destiny to obtain individual freedom and agency. These feminist jazz texts serve as prototypical examples that suggest a counterhegemonic narrative about the social and cultural impact of jazz music on women throughout the African diaspora.

Chapter 1

REUNITED

(Re)Claiming Gender in Jazz Narratives from Baldwin's "Sonny's Blues" to Angelou's "Reunion"

Maya Angelou's jazz short story "The Reunion" consists of a revision-ist narrative that attempts to reclaim a space for Black women in the jazz literary tradition. Angelou's literary re-vision can be read as what scholar Cheryl Wall describes as "worrying the line."[1] Wall notes that the popular blues trope, "worrying the line," is a technique applied "for purposes of emphasis, clarification and subversion." In appropriating the trope for critical purposes, she demonstrates that "black women's writing work similar changes on literary traditions" (Wall 8). Wall's compelling critical framework informs my reading of "The Reunion," which indicates Angelou's subversive attempts to "worry the line" of jazz literary tradition. "The Reunion" explores the bebop era, bereft of the presence of African American women improvisers, in order to provide a counternarrative that places the Black woman as central to the jazz literary tradition and jazz discourse more broadly.

"The Reunion" recalls the life of Philomena Jenkins, a virtuosic Black female piano player reminiscent of jazz pianist Mary Lou Wil-liams. Through memories and ritualized dialogue, Philomena narrates the possibility and actuality of a reunion between herself and "Beth Ann Baker of the Baker Cotton Gin." Through Philomena's first-person narrative we discover that their contentious past is steeped in the racial politics of servitude and segregation. Set in 1958, during the tail end of the bebop era, the narrative is centered on Philomena Jenkins who ultimately learns how to channel the essence of bebop in a piano solo that results in her transformation from object of denigra-tion to subject of improvisation. "The Reunion," with its insertion of jazz music and improvisation, suggests not only a meeting between two women but also the confluence of race and gender, history and memory, and at its most fundamental level, jazz and literature.

Angelou's narrative participates in what scholar Robert G. O'Meally terms "the jazz-literature correspondence."[2] O'Meally defines the jazz-literature correspondence as "the continuing effort of writers to use what they hear in jazz to give their words a jazz like quality." Based on the premise that jazz music is "styled to tell the story," he notes: "The long-standing aspiration of writers in general to capture some of the power of music in poetry and prose is evident in the vocabulary of literary analysis, much of which is derived from music" (O'Meally 535). This chapter suggests that the jazz-literature correspondence is inherent in many of Angelou's jazz texts that use music as a medium (literal, figurative, or spiritual) to allow characters to gain agency and/or subjectivity through improvisation.

From her autobiographical jazz text, *Singin' and Swingin' and Gettin' Merry Like Christmas*,[3] to her jazz short story "The Reunion," the lyrical writings of Maya Angelou are a testament to her reverence for conjoining music and literature. Written in 1976, *Singin' and Swingin'* serves as a foundation for later writings that draw our attention to her own relationship with music and, more broadly, the influence of music on Black women. In the beginning of *Singin' and Swingin'*, Angelou describes an intimate moment with music in the first few lines: "Music was my refuge. I could crawl into the spaces of the notes and curl my back to loneliness." This passage, which relates the influence of music on Angelou's life, highlights her memory of the way music protected her, embracing both her emotional and psychological state of solitude. For Angelou, music serves as a barricade to a hostile world. Music provides comfort and protection that enables her access into a safe space/place within the notes.

Further, Angelou describes her affinity for the music as if it were a lover: "In my rented room, I would play a record, then put my arms around the shoulders of the song, As we danced, glued together, I would nuzzle into its neck, kissing the skin, and rubbing its cheek with my own" (*Singin' and Swingin'* 3). It is significant to note that music is personified. With music's shoulders to wrap her arms around, legs to dance, body to be glued to, neck to kiss, and cheeks to rub against, music becomes the embodiment of desire. Although described with many characteristics of the human body, music lacks a mouth and therefore we are unable to literally and figuratively hear it. The narrator implies that although we can see the music, we cannot hear the song due to the literary medium. Thus, in this particular scenario the record becomes, like Philomena in "The Reunion," the "song struggling to be heard." Although ripe with some of the same musical venerations as *Singin' and Swingin'*, "The Reunion" suggests the historical tension between unsung women and jazz music, specifically the bebop era.

Roughly spanning the mid-1940s through the 1950s, the bebop era produced a culture of resistance represented by the music, individual style, and language of African Americans. Bebop has been called both an evolution as well as a revolution of the jazz tradition. Indeed, it can be viewed as both, as it evolved from swing in a revolutionary way. Historically, the bebop revolution has been considered a reaction to white appropriation and an attempt to render jazz music inaccessible through a coded musical language that represents the interiority of African American life and culture. In *Black Music*, Amiri Baraka underscores the significance as well as the interrelationship between African Americans and the music born of their experiences: "The song and the people is the same" and "Bop was, at a certain level of consideration, a reaction by young musicians against the sterility and formality of Swing as it moved to become a formal part of the mainstream American culture." Further, "People made Bebop" and there was a "psychological catalyst that made that music the exact registration of the social and cultural thinking of a whole generation of black Americans."[4] Yet, the social and cultural factors associated with the bebop era are usually accompanied by a masculine sensibility evidenced in the music, historical narratives, and images of the period.

In the bebop anthem "In Walked Bud," the lyrical depiction of the creation of bebop, women are absent. When reading the jazz history surrounding the bebop era, we are most likely to encounter the narratives of notable male musicians such as Charlie Parker, Dizzy Gillespie, and Thelonious Monk, to name a few. The images of the bebop era depict a masculine sense of style, which included the fashionable berets, horn-rim glasses, and the goatee.[5] In *Life* magazine, a popular photographic image of the bebop movement provides further evidence of a male-dominated era. The image is filled with private rituals, such as the depiction of a fictitious "secret handshake" between Gillespie and Benny Goodman and the coded language of Chano Pozo as he shouts "incoherently" in a "Bebop transport."[6] Culturally and socially, bebop exuded a "cool" masculinity supported by masculine images that portrayed the uber-masculine style, language, and culture of the era.

Unsurprisingly, most narratives that concern the birth of bebop exclude a female presence. The most common myth identifies the club Minton's as the place where bebop was born through the virtuosic performances of Thelonious Monk and Dizzy Gillespie, among other male musicians. This particular narrative outlining the genesis of the music, like most narratives about bebop, silences the role of Black women within this era and the influence women had on the music as well as the way in which the music affected their lives. If there was indeed a "psychological catalyst," as Baraka notes, for the creation of bebop, a music that precisely reflected the social and cultural ideology of an entire generation, then the questions that beg answers are: Was the psychological catalyst exclusive to the African American male experience? What is the relationship between this revolutionary modern jazz sound and the Black female experience? If "the song and the people is the same" and modern jazz was procreated by the people, what role did the Black woman play? Who really gave birth to modern jazz?

Significantly, a few historical counternarratives recognize Black women as co-founders of the music. The first narrative has been recounted by musician Lillian Carter (Wilson) who brings forth Josephine Boyd, a saxophonist in the all-girl band the Darlings, as a co-creator of the new sound that would eventually be known as bebop. According to Sherrie Tucker's interviews, Wilson remained adamant about the fact that Boyd "set the egg for Bebop."[7] Despite Dizzy Gillespie's inability to remember Boyd, Wilson "insisted that Boyd helped Dizzy Gillespie invent Bebop" (Tucker 206). Another counternarrative uncovers the presence of a "Mother" figure, Mary Lou Williams, as a major contributor to the construction and formation of modern jazz.

In Tammy Kernodle's *Soul on Soul: The Life and Music of Mary Lou Williams,* Williams is not only a female presence at the site of bebop's conception, but according to her own account, she helped mold and shape the sound of the music by serving as a mentor to many bebop musicians, including Charlie Christian, Bud Powell, and Thelonious Monk. Kernodle writes:

> After her nightly performances at Café Society, Mary would head uptown to a club called Minton's Playhouse on West 118th Street. It was there that this new jazz was being conceived, through the experimentations of the pianist Thelonious Monk, trumpeter Dizzy Gillespie, the drummers Kenny Clarke and Max Roach, the trombonist J.J. Johnson, and others. . . . Thelonious Monk was one of the first Beboppers to be associated with Minton's, while the other musicians, Charlie Parker, Dizzy Gillespie and Max Roach supported themselves with work for swing bands. Monk set the stage for Bebop with his complex chord changes, which few could play with him. But those who could follow Monk, such as the guitarist Charlie Christian, fed this experimentation. Mary, who had befriended Christian in the late 1930s . . . would spend countless nights with the guitarist working on compositions that explored these new approaches to jazz. . . . Of the Boppers Mary was closest to Monk, Powell, and Gillespie. But Monk, more than the others, frequently asked Mary for her musical opinion. (Kernodle 112–14)[8]

More than a female presence at the club, Williams became the "matriarch of the modern jazz movement when she opened her apartment and ears to the musical and personal concerns of the Bebop musicians" (Kernodle 114). Despite the fact that Williams played a significant role in the bebop movement, and even produced her own compositions, "she would never be viewed as an innovator in the style" (Kernodle 116). As a Black female musician within the male-dominated discourse of jazz, her dissonant narrative becomes a footnote in the historical trajectory of the revolutionary sound of bebop.[9] As a Black female musician and an innovative improviser, Williams's story becomes, like the story of her fictional equivalent Philomena Jenkins (and to a larger extent many Black female improvisers), "the song struggling to be heard." However, as a short story, "The Reunion" highlights jazz as the catalyst that enables Philomena to improvise and push the boundaries of the song to gain agency and ultimately find her voice.

Throughout "The Reunion," jazz figures prominently. Angelou underscores jazz standards from 1931 to 1958 and there seems to be a distinctive interplay between swing and bebop. "DB Blues," originally composed by Lester Young, sets the tone for the reunion that will take place between Philomena and Beth Ann. The narrative portrays how the sound of Lester Young envelops the club atmosphere as Philomena and the Cab Callen Band begin to play and "[take] off on that tune like [they] were headed for Birdland in NYC" ("The Reunion" 222). In *Being Prez: The Life and Music of Lester Young*, biographer Dave Gelly describes "DB Blues" as "secure and purposeful and packed with the surprising twists and turns that mark all of [Young's] best work. It summed up, in its quiet way a spirit of ease and freedom, of getting mellow in some little dive, of not having to wear uniform or jump out of bed at the crack of dawn" (Gelly 106).[10] With its "spirit of ease and freedom," "DB Blues" bookends the narrative. The majority of the narrative, which presents the reunion between Philomena and Beth Ann Baker, is recounted in between the "DB Blues's" "kickoff" and "release." Although the reunion is couched in between freedom and ease, it is wrought with tension. Lester Young's famous "detention barrack blues," inspired by his imprisonment in 1944, forebodes the tension that exists between the two women. Like the "ironic edge"[11] of "DB Blues," the irony of the reunion between Philomena and Beth Ann is that it occurs in the moments of disjuncture or in the breaks found throughout the narrative.

In "Improvisation and the Creative Process," music critic Albert Murray defines the break as a "disruption of the normal cadence of a piece of music." He claims that it is on the break that a musician does his/her thing. This "disjuncture" that Murray calls the moment of truth is similar to what Ralph Ellison describes as the jazz moment. It is within the jazz moment that identity is achieved and notions of individual freedom and agency are asserted. Throughout the narrative, there are multiple breaks: linguistic breaks in language indicated by the ellipses; musical breaks characterized as an interlude and jazz moment/solo; literal breaks marked by the term "intermission." It is in the break that Philomena recognizes Beth Ann; experiences her "jazz moment"; confronts Beth Ann; and finally, at the end of the short story, reaches a breakthrough. Further, the title "The Reunion" implies that there was a "break" prior to the reunification of Philomena and Beth Ann. Philomena describes her break with the Bakers: "I had lived with my parents until I was thirteen, the servants' quarters. A house behind the Baker main house. Daddy was the butler, my mother was the cook, and I went to a segregated school on the other side of town where the other kids called me the Baker Nigger" ("The Reunion" 225). Years later, when she finally sees Beth Ann with a Black man in 1958 at the Blue Palm Café, she feels incredulous.

The first line of "The Reunion" states, "Nobody could have told me that she'd be out with a black man, out, like going out" ("The Reunion" 222). During the interlude, Philomena has doubts that the young blond woman is indeed "Beth Ann Baker of the Baker Cotton Gin" but takes a second look and recalls her features: "I remember too well the turn of her cheek. The sliding way her jaw goes up to her hair. That was her" (223). The interlude allows for Philomena to gain awareness and recognition of Beth Ann and in turn, Beth Ann becomes aware of Philomena's presence through the bandleader's introduction: "Our Piano man is a lady and what a lady. A cooker and a looker. Ladies and Gentlemen, I'd like to introduce to you Miss Philomena Jenkins. Folks call her Meanie" (223).

Indeed, it is by no coincidence that Philomena is a piano player. Angelou attempts to posit Philomena as the architect of a new sound by modeling her presence on Mary Lou Williams and channeling the music of Thelonious Monk in her solo. If Williams was known to "play like a man," Philomena stands as a descendant of that tradition. Although Philomena can be read as a distinguished member of the jazz era, like Williams she is in the precarious position of being a woman in a man's world. Cal's disparaging language describes Philomena as an interloper of the jazz tradition of male piano players. Furthermore, he denigrates her on the bandstand by relegating her body to the domestic sphere, "a cooker," and reducing her to an object of the gaze, "and a looker."

It is significant that the interlude creates a space for recognition between Philomena and Beth Ann. Philomena states: "she heard my name and she looked right into my eyes. Her blue ones got as big as my black ones. She recognized me, in fact in a second we tipped eyelids at each other. Not winking. Just squinting to see better" (254). We can read this moment of recognition as the actual reunion between Philomena and Beth Ann, rather than the imagined reunion that much of the narrative explores. The reunion between jazz and women in Cal's introduction relates to the reunion between Beth Ann and Philomena. Both of these reunions allow for the confluence of history and memory. Sitting on the bandstand, Philomena remains preoccupied with the physical presence of Beth Ann until the next song, "Round 'Bout Midnight," compels her to remember her own subjectivity:

["Round 'Bout Midnight"] used to be my song, for so many reasons. In Baker, the only time I could practice jazz, in the church, was round 'bout midnight. When the best chord changes came to me it was generally round 'bout midnight. When my first lover held me in his arms, it was round 'bout midnight. Usually when its time to play that tune I dig right in it. But this time I was too busy thinking about Beth and her family . . . and what she was doing in Chicago, on the South Side, escorted by the grooviest looking cat I'd seen in a long time. I was really trying to figure it out, then Cal's saxophone pushed its way into my figurings. Forced me to remember "Round 'Bout Midnight." ("The Reunion" 224)

It is the music that moves Philomena to remember her past. As Cheryl Wall notes, "music is at once the container and transmitter of memory" (Wall 10). It is noteworthy that the title of the song is mentioned three times and used literally, which suggests Angelou's play on language. The repetition of "Round 'Bout Midnight" can seemingly allude to two musical references and one personal. Musically, it can be read as referring to the song "'Round Midnight," a jazz standard popularized by Thelonious Monk in 1944. Alternatively, one can read it as a play on Miles Davis's debut hard bop album, released in 1957. Lastly, its personal reference indicates the narrator's own revision of not only the title but also the way in which she improvises on the tune.

Philomena's jazz moment takes place within her solo performance of the fictionalized bebop tune "Round 'Bout Midnight." Her jazz moment of improvisation is rooted in both history and memory as the song reminds her of the "years of loneliness, the doing without days, the C.M.E. church, and the old ladies with hands like men and the round 'bout dreams of crossing over Jordan" ("The Reunion" 224). This memory propels her to action:

> Then I took thirty-two bars. My fingers found the places be-
> tween the keys where the blues and the truth lay hiding. I dug
> out the story of a woman without a man, and a man without
> hope. I tried to wedge myself in and lay down in the groove
> between B-flat and B-natural. I must of gotten close to it, be-
> cause the audience brought me out with their clapping. Even
> Cal said, "Yeah baby, that's it." I nodded to him then to the audi-
> ence and looked around for Beth. ("The Reunion" 255)

Here, the phrase "then I took" suggests appropriation as well as pos-session of the music. Philomena's identity seems to hide in between "the blues and the truth." Her attempt to reach that place, and in effect assert her own identity and subjectivity, lives in this moment of improvisation. Improvisation surrounds the solo as her hands are described as disembodied, "finding" their place in the ephemeral co-vert space where the blues and truth exist. This space tells the story of historical trauma rooted in the days of slavery as Black women and men were denied hope. Digging deeper into the music and de-scending, like Ellison's Invisible Man, into the "depths of the music," Philomena attempts to "lay down in the groove between B-flat and B-natural."

Far into the music, suspended in an otherworldly and out-of-body experience, the sound of applause takes Philomena out of her trance. Cal's affirmation "Yeah baby, that's it" confirms that she indeed has become one with the music, achieving her own sound and "saying something." Within this jazz moment of improvisation, Philomena asserts her identity and subjectivity by responding to Beth Ann's gaze and showing her that she is no longer her "flunky" but rather a creative innovator with the ability to improvise and "say something nobody else can say" (225). By virtue of her ability to improvise, she becomes a jazz woman of the tradition, resisting the boundaries set forth for female musicians at the time.

However, Philomema's solo, serving as a response to Beth Ann, falls on deaf ears as "Beth was gone. So was her boyfriend" (224). Beth Ann's absence compels Philomena to dig deeper into her past. Through Philomena's interior monologue, readers discover the hostile past the two women share. Here we find the oral tradition of storytelling as Philomena recounts her memories. Philomena's (re)memory of Beth Ann is both specific and painful. Philomena remembers "shak[ing] farts out of her sheets, wash[ing]her dirty drawers and pick[ing] up after her slovenly mother. . . ." Philomena was still "aching from the hurt Georgia put on [her]" (224). Growing up in the segregated South, Philomena lived with her parents in the servants' quarters behind Beth Ann's house. The memory of a segregated school on the "other side of town," enduring the taunts of school-aged children calling her "the Baker Nigger," and being forced to wear Beth's "hand-me-down" clothes remains emblazoned in her mind. Philomena remarks, "I had a lot to say to Beth, and she was gone" (225). The language that is overheard by readers in Philomena's interior monologue contrasts with Philomena's musical conversation with the band.

Philomena seems capable of articulating the complexity of her feelings only through the music. As the band continues with the rest of the set, Philomena performs some of her "favorite" tunes, "Sophisticated Lady," "Misty" and "Cool Blues," which show the range of her virtuosic capabilities. Yet she does not "get back into the groove until . . . 'When your lover has gone.'" Here the musical language of the solo and the subsequent songs within the set contrast with actual conversational language. Philomena's ability to articulate herself through the music parallels her silence when Beth Ann returns to the club during intermission and approaches her. Philomena recalls: "I couldn't think of anything to say. Did I remember her? There was no way I could answer the question" (226).

Philomena's silence as well as her gaze serves as an inarticulate response. Angelou uses the inarticulate gaze as a literary convention that serves as a substitute for a verbal response. Thus Philomena spends the majority of the conversation looking at Beth through the "mirror over the bar." For Philomena, interacting with Beth through the mirror is "not threatening at all" (226). She listens to Beth Ann go on about her relationship with her Black male companion Willard, and how Beth Ann's parents disapprove of their pending marriage. Beth Ann states, "Willard is the first thing I ever got for myself. And I'm not going to give him up" (227). Philomena says nothing until she is moved by the sound of the band getting ready for the next set: "the musicians were tuning up on the bandstand. [She] drained [her] glass and stood" (227). After Beth Ann invites her to her wedding for which she does not have a date or a place, Philomena retorts, "Goodbye Beth. Tell your parents I said go to hell and take you with them for company" (228).

Philomena then proceeds to the bandstand and contemplates the reality of their encounter as she sits at the piano. She thinks of "everything" that Beth holds by virtue of her race and economic status; yet, "halfway into the DB Blues release" she remarks that although Beth Ann accumulated the money, she possessed the music. For Philomena, the music becomes the more valued treasure, priceless even as it has the ability to bring her to new heights "up high above them." The "DB Blues Release" anticipates her breakthrough as she comes to the conclusion that, "No matter how bad times became I would always be the song struggling to be heard" and begins to cry: "The piano keys were slippery with tears. I know, I sure as hell wasn't crying for myself" (228). Her tears are a form of emotional release, a physical sign of her emotional power to mourn her past yet move beyond it toward her future. In this final scene, she is crying for Beth Ann as well as the Black female collective that Philomena represents. For Philomena, the Black woman will always be the song struggling to be heard, until she comes to voice.

The song struggling to be heard is the woman's narrative in jazz discourse. Although this song began within a male-dominated matrix that silenced the Black female voice, Angelou enables us to hear Philomena's resounding cry throughout the jazz text. Thus Philomena's assertion that she "will always be the song struggling to be heard," is challenged by means of her evocative narrative and our critical engagement with it. If "the song struggling to be heard" is indeed the story of Black women improvisers within jazz literary tradition, then "The Reunion," read as a jazz text, becomes a "site"[12] or a repository for the cultural memory of African American women and jazz music.

The jazz text speaks to the disjuncture where jazz music conjoins with gender, and Black female resistance becomes a by-product of the revolutionary bebop era. Thus within the jazz text, what remains true to form is Ralph Ellison's contention that "this familiar music demanded action." This statement speaks to the end goal of these revisionist jazz texts as music serves as the catalyst for the various improvisational acts of assertion. The moment of improvisation in the text, because it is couched within a moment of hostility or violence, becomes a moment of protest that enables individual assertion and ultimately leads to freedom. The effect of the jazz moment of improvisation debunks our traditional view of improvisation and redefines it, within the context of the jazz text, as a cultural form of resistance.

Angelou's narrative exemplifies the "action" demanded by the familiar music: to reclaim the past and give hope for the future by uncovering the "power and the pain of historical memory" (Wall 22). In essence, Philomena's narrative song, like other female narratives both past and present, improvise a space within the jazz literary tradition as an alternative melody that resounds within, as it unsettles, jazz discourse.

MUSICAL SIGNIFYIN(G)

A Theory of Cry and Response
in Gayl Jones's *Corregidora*

Gayl Jones's *Corregidora* is a complex portrait of the traumatic effects of slavery on generations of women. The female body remains central to the narrative, as women are admonished to reproduce and make generations so that they can bear witness to their history. The novel centers on Ursa Corregidora's inability to bear children because her husband, Mutt, has caused her to fall down a flight of stairs, leaving her barren. The narrative engages us with an underlying rhythm of slavery and a central melody of unrequited love as it becomes a complex solo of past memories infused into present realities, all forging a path to self-discovery for the lost blues singer, Ursa.

Various scholars and critics have remarked on the blues aesthetic in the novel.[1] Scholar Claudia Tate asserts that "ultimately, the blues is Ursa's finest creation; it is the surrogate daughter who bears witness to both Corregidora's legacy and Ursa's indomitable will to free herself from the tyranny of historical oppression" (*Corregidora* 141). Similarly, Donia Allen examines the formal devices of the blues—"repetition, call-and-response, and the blues break"—to "reveal crucial aspects of [Jones's] characters' lives and struggles as well as important themes in [Jones's] work in general" (Allen 257). Although these articles make compelling arguments for the blues within the narrative, they fail to examine the nuanced presence of jazz. To the extent that the novel uses blues to foreground a historical past, it also introduces jazz through the ritualized dialogue of cry-and-response, constructs Ursa into a Wild Woman spectacle who becomes the subject rather than the object of the gaze, and uncovers the jazz moment of improvisation at the end of the novel via language that echoes freedom and the possibility for renewal. Because *Corregidora* is most predominantly read as a blues text, many critics miss how jazz surrounds the text. By overlooking the significance of jazz and its relationship to the women in the novel, the mystery of the narrative's central issue—how Ursa will make generations without the ability to reproduce—remains unresolved.

This chapter examines how Jones interweaves a jazz ethos into her quintessentially blues text. Rereading the text through a jazz lens enables the reader to distinguish the blues text from the jazz text and marks the relationship between jazz and narrative form. I examine the musical qualities surrounding the rhetorical motif of cry-and-response and investigate the ambiguous ending of the novel by exploring whether Ursa's quest for ultimate freedom within the jazz moment is ever realized.

Jones's own distinction between the jazz text and the blues text helps question the critical reception of *Corregidora* as a blues narrative by connecting the ambiguities of language in the text to a jazz aesthetic. In *Liberating Voices: Oral Tradition in African American Literature*,[2] Jones explains that, although jazz and blues texts are similar, they have defining features that differentiate them:

> The jazz text is generally more complex and sophisticated than blues text in its harmonies, rhythms, and surface structure. . . . Jazz text is stronger in its accents; its vocabulary and syntax is often more convoluted and ambiguous than blues. It is often more difficult to read than a blues text, tending to abstractions over concreteness of detail. It shares with a blues text a sense of extemporaneity in its fluid rhythmical design and syncopated understructure, its sound and meaning systems, its rejection of duality. Jazz texts tend to have a faster pace and tempo than a blues text. (*Liberating Voices* 200)

Given Jones's definition, I focus on the two predominant distinguishing qualities of the jazz text: its complex narrative form/surface structure and its convoluted and ambiguous language/vocabulary and syntax. In addition, I believe that the jazz text incorporates moments of improvisation that serve as defining moments for the protagonist.

Based on these distinguishing qualities, *Corregidora* constitutes a jazz text rather than a blues text. Further, jazz's musical components correspond with the way in which these qualities function throughout the text: antagonistic cooperation, which characterizes jazz's distinctive musical social organization in performance, describes the novel's narrative form; cry-and-response—a rhetorical motif that reflects the musical, nonlinguistic dialogue between instruments—describes the ambiguous and convoluted language found in the ritualized dialogue of the jazz text; and the jazz moment of improvisation, understood musically as the space within the music where an improvised solo takes place, appears similarly within the text as a self-defining improvised moment of assertion that produces both agency and freedom.

The narrative organization of *Corregidora* can be read through what scholar John Szwed calls the "musical social organization" of jazz. In *Jazz 101*, Szwed notes:

> Jazz has a distinctive musical social organization in performance. Jazz musicians play against as well as with other jazz musicians, working one rhythm or melody against another competitively but also reciprocally. It's what Ralph Ellison called the cruel contradiction implicit in the music, the individual finding personal identity against and with the group. Individual musicians assert themselves in solos, but other musicians may enter into each other's solos, not so much as an interruption but as a gesture of support and attentiveness. Jazz at its most complex—say, during collectively improvised playing—calls on the musicians to play with unique voices, to sound like no one else, and yet at the same time to cohere as one, with a single goal. (Szwed 56–57)

This musical organization can be used as a metaphor for the narrative construction of Jones's text. According to Ellison, people are individuals yet part of the collective; although they survive on and due to "shit, grit, and mother wit," their being always exists in relation to others, especially with regard to jazz group dynamics. Jazz musicians are also encouraged to "tell the story," an idea central to *Corregidora*'s narrative, as four generations of women riff on the improvised oral narrative of Corregidora, the Portuguese slave breeder that haunts the novel. All of the women in the novel use their own melodies or voices to convey their stories of love, hate, and loss as they relate to past relationships with men and Corregidora specifically. These stories directly and indirectly relate to the underlying narrative rhythm of slavery. As Ursa explains, "my great-grandmama told my grandmama the part she lived through that my grandmama didn't live through and my grandmama told my mama what they both lived through and my mama told me what they all lived through and we were suppose to pass it down like that from generation to generation so we'd never forget" (*Corregidora* 9). Improvisation in this particular narrative of slavery entails repetition and reconfiguration as we hear Great Gram's story through the voice of Ursa and Ursa's grandmother's story through the voice of Irene. Although the narrative is told from Ursa's point of view, there are breaks that enable other characters to solo and incorporate their own views. These narrative breaks are marked with italicized words—that is, italics distinguish past narratives of slavery and Ursa's current condition of enslavement. Italics thus visually divide the narrative into various spaces and eras, allowing readers to compare and contrast the narratives of the past and present.

Jones also uses the visual breaks in narrative to distinguish Ursa's narrative voice from the voices of her past. The underlying narrative—Corregidora's breeding of and illicit sexual relations with his own offspring—seem an allusion to the historicized objectification of the Black female body during slavery. Black feminist scholars such as Patricia Hill Collins and Deborah McDowell analyze the issue of Black women's historical trauma and assert that the ability to come to voice allows for a sort of healing through the reinvention/retelling of the female slave narrative.

Collins contends that "rape and other acts of overt violence that Black women have experienced, such as physical assault during slavery, domestic abuse, incest and sexual extortion, accompany Black women's subordination in a system of race, class, and gender oppression" (Collins 177). As a response to this systematic oppression, these women attempt to obtain a form of agency by narrating their own stories aloud to their offspring. If the narrative involves improvisation, repetition, and allusion, then it must also undergo revision. Ursa uses improvisation to describe the narrative of old man Corregidora to Tadpole, internally questioning the moniker that describes him:

> Old man Corregidora, the Portuguese slave breeder and whore-
> monger. (Is that what they call them?) He fucked his own
> whores and fathered his own breed. They did the fucking and
> had to bring him the money they made. My grandmama was
> his daughter, but he was fucking her too. She said when they
> did away with slavery down there they burned all the slavery
> papers so it would be like they never had it. (9)

Here, Ursa begins to doubt her own memory of Corregidora, using improvisation to fill in the gaps about what she has forgotten. Her rhetorical question, placed in parentheses, signifies an internal mono-logue that Tadpole does not hear yet to which readers are privy. This internal monologue suggests that in passing along the story, Ursa has inserted her own language and consequently redefined Corregidora as a whoremonger rather than a slave owner. Ursa's uncertainty also exposes the fallacy of memory as it relates to passing on/down oral histories. This moment ultimately raises questions about the authen-ticity of such narratives and emphasizes Ursa's ability to improvise on various aspects of the story.

The stories told to Ursa through the voices of Great Gram, Gram, and Irene are simultaneously individual and part of the collective memory that must be used to leave evidence. Ursa is improvising her own solo by placing a label on Corregidora yet cohering as part of the larger goal: "The important thing is making generations. They can burn the papers but they can't burn conscious, Ursa. And that what makes the evidence. And that's what makes the verdict" (*Corregidora* 22). Indeed, the command to "make generations" and "leave evidence" is repeated throughout the novel. The improvised repetition of the command from generation to generation and its ultimate reconfigu-ration through Ursa can be read through a feminist lens as well as within a psychoanalytic framework.

The repetition of the command to "make generations" relates to what Sigmund Freud terms a repetition-compulsion in his essay "Beyond the Pleasure Principle." According to Freud, the repetition-compulsion is "the mind's tendency to repeat traumatic events in order to deal with them." Freud explains further that "the repetition can take the form of dreams, storytelling, or even hallucination." For Ursa, the repetition-compulsion takes all three forms: Ursa dreams of giving birth to Corregidora, repeats the story throughout the narrative, and experiences hallucinations about bearing the next generation. This repetition-compulsion and her inability to sing the blues after the fall make Ursa a hysterical subject, following in the tradition of past generations.

After the fall, Ursa begins to suffer from suppressed hysteria. The loss of her voice corresponds to the dispossession of the female body. She thinks of her ancestors, "the girl who had to sleep with her master and mistress. Her father, the master. Her daughter's father. The father of her daughter's daughter . . . days that were pages of hysteria. Their survival depended on suppressed hysteria" (*Corregidora* 59). Jacques Lacan describes the hysterical subject as lacking in being, a subject who "wants to be" (Lacan 29). In "The Subject and the Other," scholar Colette Soler describes the hysterical subject as feeling "his or her own lack and suffers from it . . . the hysterical subject is searching for a sense or feeling of being . . . and to have this feeling of being is to be loved or more precisely to be desired" (Soler, 50–51). Because Ursa lacks the ability to articulate what she calls "all those blues feelings" and can no longer express her "feeling ways" (50), she cannot come to terms with her emotions or how she is supposed to feel about the events that make up her past.

What distinguishes Ursa from past generations is her ability to sing the blues. After the fall, Ursa's blues became more potent; her voice became "new" (*Corregidora* 50) and her sound was "hard" (96). Cat, a close friend, remarks that Ursa sounds like she has "been through something. Because Ursa's voice has changed, her songs take on a different meaning. Although Ursa relies on the language of the blues, her voice reveals that something more is at stake. In an attempt to describe how she feels—what she calls her "feeling ways" (50)—she tells her mother that she is "trying to explain it in blues, without words, the explanation somewhere behind the words" (66). What is she trying to articulate? How will she explain it without words? If Ursa's narrative is based on her "feeling ways" and the interpretation or explanation of those feeling ways lies somewhere behind the language of the blues, it becomes necessary to move beyond the surface meaning of the words Ursa includes in her blues-like stanzas. What Ursa is trying to explain—the freedom inherent in finding one's voice—is expressed in the complex ritualized dialogue of cry-and-response.

Throughout the text, there is an explicit tension between what is spoken and what is written, what is said and what is heard, what is articulated and what is silenced. In an interview, Jones makes clear that she is experimenting with a lot of oral traditional forms: "All experimenting involves language, but language with a lot of different connections, not just changing words and the syntax of sentencing in an obvious way. Many times it has to do with the relationship between the words and the people hearing the words, and not just the relationship between the words themselves" (qtd. in Harper 359). Jones reconfigures Ursa's dialogue to denote her internal struggle to articulate her desires through language. Ursa's ritualized dialogue demonstrates the transformation of language in terms of time and space, past and present, reality and memory.

The rhetorical structure of call-and-response seems complicated by the cry in ritualized dialogue. The distinction between the call and the cry has historical roots in African American music as well as communication. The call derives from the cry, yet they serve different functions. The call is a type of cry "which asks for something for or from someone else" or "pronounces judgment," while cries are expressions of "deeply felt emotional experience" (James 18). According to musical scholar Ashenafi Kebede in *Roots of Black Music*, calls remain synonymous with hollers and whoopin' yet different from cries: "Calls are primarily used to communicate messages, [while] cries express a deeply felt emotional experience. . . . [T]hey are half-sung and half-yelled" (Kebede 130). Musicologist Willis James defines a cry as "an instant reminder of the primitive. It is the oldest form of vocal expression. From it arises all of the things associated with speech and musical tone concepts" (James 17). Moreover, James maintains that a cry, whether articulate or inarticulate, has an enigmatic aspect, "a certain something in it that says more than mere words can express" (18). Decoding the cry-and-response dialogue permits an exploration of the complex issues that haunt Ursa.

Jones deploys jazz devices such as the break, repetition, and improvisation to underscore moments that take language out of the
realm of call-and-response and into a ritualized cry-and-response
dialogue. According to Jones, ritualistic dialogue contains three
elements: "the language, the rhythm of the people talking, and the
rhythm between the people talking" (qtd. in Harper 359). For Jones,
the "communication of thoughts and feelings through a system of
arbitrary signals, such as voice sounds, gestures, or written symbols,"
remains the key to ritualized dialogue (359). Dialogue can be taken
out of the realm of call-and-response by "creat[ing] a rhythm that
people wouldn't ordinarily use in real talk, although they are saying
the words they might ordinarily use [doing] something to the rhythm
or something to the words. . . . [B]oth things take the dialogue out of
the naturalistic realm—change its quality" (359). Jones's experiment
with removing dialogue from its naturalistic realm ultimately complicates the rhetorical structure of call-and-response and consequently
creates a ritualized dialogue of cry-and-response. By complicating
the rhetorical structure, Jones produces moments of ambiguity and
misunderstanding not only for readers but also for the characters.

Unlike cry-and-response, call-and-response can be clearly identified because it follows a particular pattern. When Ursa calls, someone
responds; the call is then repeated, and the final response is a verbal
resolution. An example of a call-and-response exchange can be seen
in Ursa's dialogue with Cat about whether Mutt really loved Ursa:

> "If that nigger love me he wouldn't've throwed me down the
> steps," I called.
> "What?" She came to the door.
> "I said if that nigger loved me he wouldn't've throwed me
> down the steps."
> "I know niggers love you do worse than that," she said.
> (36–37)

Here, Ursa attempts to explain to Cat that there should be a distinction between love and violence. If Mutt loved her, then he would
not physically abuse her. Cat's reply, that Ursa's claim is wrong and
that love often entails far worse violence, is characteristic of the love

relationships throughout the text. This call-and-response dialogue bears a clear verbal format: a call is made, a response is posed, then a recall (a repetition of the call with clarification), and finally a verbal resolution. This pattern appears like the traditional blues stanza. A cry-and-response dialogue expresses a marked difference: the cry includes something beyond mere words. The cry-and-response dialogues occur during intimate moments and involve misinterpretation and ambiguity.

In *Corregidora*, the cry sounds both articulate and inarticulate. Although the cry is usually surrounded by language, it is a musical signifier of inarticulacies: the meaning of the inarticulate cry stands outside of language. Some examples of inarticulate cries are characterized by silences, hard gazes, "low crying," and screams. Unlike call-and-response, the cry-and-response dialogue is usually resolved through a physical rather than verbal line of resolution. That is, the narrative depicts an action that follows or will follow the dialogue rather than a verbal response that represents a resolution. Cry-and-response often occurs within the context of a private sexualized moment and involves tension between the speakers. Ursa's cries take place as she attempts to explain her "feeling ways," usually within a private dialogue.

Corregidora begins with a cry-and-response dialogue between Ursa and Mutt that sets the stage. After Ursa's performance at Happy's Café, her inability to understand Mutt's cry leads to the tragic fall that leaves her barren. The dialogue begins with Mutt's cry:

"I don't like those mens messing with you." he said.
"Don't nobody mess with me."
"Mess with they eyes."
That was when I fell. (1)

This dialogue presents the ambiguity of language and the physical act, Ursa's fall, which provides the impetus to Ursa's written narrative, since it prevents her from singing her story and thus forces her to write it. Ursa cries back to Mutt after he vents his discontent with the way in which the taxonomic gaze of her predominantly male audience objectifies her. The reference to the eyes recurs as a theme, conveying meaning as well as a response. Ursa often gives a "hard look" as a response during a cry-and-response dialogue. Ursa also takes people in with her eyes as they watch her sing the blues on stage. This dialogue contains two significant aspects: language/voice and the gaze. Ursa's Wild Woman status is represented vis-à-vis her voice and the gaze. The language of the cry-and-response seems to be bound to what Lacan describes in *The Four Fundamental Concepts* as *meconnaissance*, a "failure to recognize or a misconstruction" (Lacan 281). Neither Mutt nor Ursa understands the innate fallacy of language, and both of them misconstruct the term *mess*. The cries are discordant because of the boundless signifiers attached to the word. Ursa understands *mess* to mean to bother or antagonize physically, while Mutt defines it in terms of mental and visual objectification. Unerringly, the eyes are used to witness as well as perform acts of violation.

In "'I Hear You with My Eyes'; or, The Invisible Master," scholar Slavoj Žižek notes that the "voice and the gaze are the two objects added by Jacques Lacan to the list of Freudian 'partial objects' (breast, feces, phallus). They are objects, that is to say, they are not on the side of the looking/hearing subject but on the side of what the subject sees or hears" (Žižek 90).[3] Ursa represents the object that lures the gaze toward her. As a blues singer, she is in the spotlight, and all eyes are always already gazing at her. But Ursa returns the gaze as they watch her sing the blues on stage. The voice and the gaze are inextricably woven together; as Ursa states, the audience "watched me. I felt as if they could see my feelings somewhere in the bottom of my eyes" (*Corregidora* 51). Ursa looks mysterious and alluring as she stands on stage. She allows the crowd to "see" her (in the sense of view her) but not to "see" her (understand her). In essence, because the audience is unable to truly see all of her, a blind spot is formed, and it can be filled only through understanding Ursa's blues. Ursa attempts to make her audience understand her "feeling ways" by screaming—a cry of agony. This cry expresses an attempt to inform the audience of her pain: "It was as if I wanted them to see what [Mutt] had done, hear it. . . . My voice felt like it was screaming" (50). Ursa brings forth the cry in a dialogue with the audience. This coded cry/scream becomes the telling inarticulacy that allows Ursa to go beyond the music and reveal her pain in "blues, somewhere behind the words."

Another Wild Woman in the novel, Cat Lawson, also uses the coded language of cry-and-response. One of the novel's most cryptic dialogues takes place between Cat and her young lover, Jeffy. Cat is exhibits a fluid sexuality as she engages with both men and women. Ursa learns about Cat's queer identity when she overhears a conversation between Cat and Jeffy. The dialogue takes place behind closed doors, meaning that Ursa can report only what she hears, not what she can see. Cat begins the ritualized dialogue:

> "If you bother her again I'll give you a fist to fuck."
>> "I ain't going to bother her again."
> "I said if you do you got my fist to fuck."
> Then there was silence.
> "I could've told you she wouldn't."
> "What? You ask her?"
> There was a loud slap, and then low crying.
> "Laugh now."
> "Please, Miss Catherine."
> "I said, 'Laugh now.'"
> Low crying.
> "I didn't go in there to do it. I must've did it in my sleep."
> "Shit if you did."
> Silence.
> "Shit."
> "Hush."
> I had eased back to the door and by the time the "hush" came, I'd stepped back into the bedroom. (47)

Similar to previous ritualized cry-and-response dialogues, this conversation operates within an intimate moment and suggests power on the part of the dominating sexual figure Cat. Like the male figures in the narrative, Cat is characterized in the position of power due to the brash, violent language with which she threatens Jeffy. Cat's threat, "I'll give you a fist to fuck," sounds reminiscent of the hard-knuckled way in which men push the act of sex throughout the text.

Jones puts the Wild Woman into a masculinist discourse of the violence and abuse inherent in heterosexual love relationships, where women are usually the victims and men are the victimizers. Cat's protectively violent voice as she threatens Jeffy into submission sounds reminiscent of the voices of Tadpole and Mutt. Jones creates a cry-and-response dialogue within this homoerotic moment to suggest that power dynamics exist outside gender boundaries and heteronormative relationships. Further, within any type of love relationship, victimizers reinforce the measure of power they impose through the possession and enactment of violent language or action.

Jeffy's "low crying" after Cat's threat implies both vulnerability and fear, serving as Jeffy's response as she echoes the inarticulate language of acquiescence. Her cry also echoes that of Ursa, yet it is distinguished from Ursa's in that Jeffy does not stifle her cries, as Ursa often does, but allows them to relay a message to the intended listener. Telling inarticulacies or coded language were propagated by the women in the community, as evidenced in the abstract dialogue between women.

Jones's insertion of a homoerotic subplot speaks to the divided nature of the novel's community of women. Cat's refusal to reveal her identity to Ursa suggests the tension that exists around the topic of female relationships. Ursa does not support Cat's lesbian identity for fear of becoming like her, but nevertheless remains loyal to Cat by not exposing her to the community. Jones makes clear that regardless of sexuality, women were forced to suppress their erotic tendencies to conform to social codes of conduct vis-à-vis an outwardly explicit heteronormative femininity. That Jones chooses to reveal Cat's identity through an overheard and ambiguous cry-and-response dialogue refers back to the difficulty of understanding such a dialogue.

The ritualized cry-and-response dialogue between Tadpole and Ursa follows a similar pattern of ambiguity, misinterpretation, and physical action/resolution. Like all the romantic relationships in the text, the initiator of the ritualized cry is in the position of master and asserts control and power over the other. In a sexual dialogue with her second husband, Tadpole McCormick, Ursa's derisive cry reveals her vulnerability and inability to sexually connect with him. However, because he is just a figure for the moment who does not occupy a permanent position in her world, their communication, both sexual and verbal, becomes stifled and bereft of possibilities. As Ursa describes their intimate dialogue:

> We stood up but I couldn't get him inside me. I wanted to say, "I'm not relaxed enough," but I didn't. He stroked me on the behind, pulling up on me, then he said, "You have to work too." He pulled up on me more, squatting down. He took me with him to the wall, squatting more. I still couldn't get him in.
> "Work, Ursa."
> "I am working," I said. It was almost a cry, but a cry I didn't want him to hear. I don't know how long it was between it and when I finally said, "Tadpole, I can't, I can't." (83)

The rhythmic breaks in this dialogue are filled with movement. The rhythm between the people talking is disrupted and displaced by the sexual movement being performed. Both movement and speech are significant. Tadpole's initial call is physical, as he attempts to enter Ursa. Her response, which remains in her subconscious, is that she is not "relaxed" enough. Thus, their attempt to physically commune is thwarted by Ursa's mental as well as physical state.

Her inability to communicate the truth to him blocks the forced connection they are attempting to create. Tadpole's command, "Work, Ursa," is countered by Ursa's cry, "I am working," which is only expressed halfway because she does not want Tadpole to hear and therefore understand its underlying meaning. Because of the physical movement and exertion, the sexual moment is constructed as work. Ursa's cry seems coded to mean that sex with Tadpole is actual work, something that she feels obligated to do. But Tadpole misinterprets the cry to mean that she is trying, and Tadpole's resolution is physical—he continues his attempt at sexual intimacy. Had it been a full cry, perhaps he would have understood the coded language and stopped, but he continues until she plainly declares that she can no longer continue and physically stops.

This sexual experience, like its predecessors, presents a critical emotional state for Ursa. Sex as work alludes to Great Gram and Gram as Corregidora's whores and points to the commodification of the Black female body. A kind of violence is thus inherent in this moment as Tadpole attempts to force his way into Ursa. Her movements become contrived as she forces herself to perform and represses her cry.

Throughout the text, Ursa is constantly repressing the cry and replacing it with her blues voice. Thus, every blues form or stanza replaces a moment of emotional feeling. She literally sings to keep from crying. When asked when she sings the blues, Ursa replies, "Everytime I ever want to cry, I sing the blues" (46). Thus, we see the blues interrupted by the literal cry in the blues-like dialogue at the end. This break in language is also a breakthrough for Ursa. Her tears, which she often describes as "soot crying out of [her] eyes" (66), express a form of emotional release, the only physical sign of her emotional power to mourn her past yet move beyond it toward her future.

The novel's last ritualistic dialogue conveys Ursa's attempt to reconcile her relationship with Mutt as well as reconfigure what it means for her to bear witness to future generations. Returning home to the Drake Hotel with Mutt, Ursa remarks that although it was the same place and the same feel of the place, it was not the same room (184). Although Ursa is in the same place, her sense of who she is in relation to Mutt seems very different. Twenty years later, although they are still in dialogue, Ursa can finally articulate a response. Leaning back and "pulling [Ursa] up by the shoulders," Mutt begins:

"I don't want a kind of woman that hurt you," he said.

"Then you don't want me."

"I don't want a kind of woman that hurt you."

"Then you don't want me."

"I don't want a kind of woman that hurt you."

"Then you don't want me."

He shook me till I fell against him crying. "I don't want a kind of man that'll hurt me neither," I said.

He held me tight. (185)

After the novel's cry-and-response patterns, this passage suggests that the term *woman*, repeated three times, alludes to the generations of women who form Ursa's matriarchal lineage. Although Ursa acknowledges that she is born into a history that she cannot change, she also realizes that she is not "Corregidora's daughter" (103). Nevertheless, she remains a descendant and a product of the "kind of woman" Mutt does not want. Ursa's final statement suggests a type of interdependence as it relates to their relationship. If she is not to be that "kind of woman," he cannot be that "kind of man." Here, Jones suggests that the historical trauma of Corregidora, fueled with hate and abuse of Black women, created the kind of women who hurt each other, as evidenced through the stories of Great Gram and Gram. In effect, Ursa's call sounds an attempt to force Mutt to take ownership of his own role in producing the kind of woman who can reciprocate love rather than repeat the hurt.

Ursa's final cry-and-response dialogue can also be interpreted within the context of what anthropologist Greg Urban calls Amerindian Brazilian ritual wailing, which ranges from fully expressive to expressive-descriptive. Wailing entails a process of making public the feelings of the person who is wailing. It is intended not to be heard in the ordinary linguistic sense but rather to be overheard. As Urban notes, ritual wailing carries an overt function and an actual function for the person who engages in it: "Ritual wailing purports overtly not to engage an addressee, but to allow anyone within earshot access to something that would otherwise be private" (Urban 386). The actual function is "undoubtedly communicative—to let other members of the community know that the individual has the proper orientation to the dead person, visitor, or whatever life situation occasions the wailing. It is a kind of calculated accident, an action designed to appear spontaneous" (Urban 386).

Ursa's ritual wailing occurs within a private sexualized moment that is connected to her great-grandmother's private memory of what she did to Corregidora that could make him "want to kill her" (184). Ursa discovers the answer to this question during a sexually intimate reunion with Mutt. Great Gram must have been in a position in which she had the power to determine whether Corregidora lived or died.

The discovery of Great Gram's private memory mirrors Ursa's own struggle for power with Mutt.

The balance of power between Ursa and Mutt shifts when Ursa takes on the dominant role and asserts herself. This assertion is first seen when Ursa performs fellatio on Mutt, a form of inarticulate communication: "I knew what he wanted, I wanted it too. We didn't speak" (184). Ursa's ingestion of Mutt's semen suggests the transference of power as the phallus becomes weak and limp and the mouth is impregnated with life-giving semen. With this act, Jones redefines Mutt and Ursa's relationship. Ursa puts herself in an animalistic position, on her knees and holding onto Mutt's ankles. Although Mutt is physically above her, she remains in the position of power as a consequence of her sexual control over Mutt. During this act of fellatio, she connects her relationship to that between Great Gram and Corregidora. Ursa finally feels in control, realizing that she could "kill him" (184). In this powerful position, Ursa understands that she has the ability to sever his genitalia, just as Jones depicts Davis's murder in her second novel, *Eva's Man*. However, instead of using her mouth to castrate Mutt, Ursa decides to use her voice and assert her control through her final ritualized cry, where she is physically on top and Mutt is beneath her.

Ursa chooses to articulate her needs in what scholar Cynthia Smith describes as a "song that provides the novel's resolution creat[ing] a new pattern; instead of two repeated lines, there are three: one for each generation before Ursa, who in the resolution is able to renounce the old pattern of bondage and pain" (Smith 238). Ursa's cry-and-response dialogue also evokes not only a verbal response but also a physical reaction from Mutt. As Urban notes, "ritual wailing can motivate others to action, through kindling in them either the emotion of grief or the desire to display that they too have the socially appropriate sentiment. . . . [O]ne person wailing may stimulate others to do so, resulting in a veritable chorus. . . . The crying, when it is performed by various persons, men and women, frequently has the character of true duets" (Urban 387).

Thus Ursa and Mutt's cry-and-response dialogue reads like a duet: As Smith concludes, "Instead of a single voice bearing witness to anguish and pain, there are two in an exchange that brings about healing and reconciliation." Ursa's final line, "I don't want a man that will hurt me either," which precedes Mutt's act of holding her, defines her jazz moment, as she asserts herself and states her demands. The exchange enables both Mutt and Ursa to redefine who they are and who they will be to one another. Ursa gains subjectivity through her final cry as she reconfigures what she needs to make generations.

For Ursa, that act of making generations does not have to be actualized solely through procreation. In replacement for the vagina, Ursa's mouth becomes the tool that allows her to make generations. Her improvised solo, "I don't want no man that'll hurt me" (185), can be described as her moment of truth. In Ursa's last cry, she risks losing Mutt by asserting her own needs. Similarly, this moment prompts her only opportunity to reconfigure the master/slave dynamic that has characterized the relationships of all the women in her past. Mutt embraces Ursa's vow to reconfigure her destiny as he holds her tightly.

Ursa's jazz moment of individual assertion lives within the symbolic break in language, the disjuncture between what is verbally represented and what actually exists. Ursa's heroic moment comes with passing *on* Corregidora's story through the act of storytelling and an attempt to *pass* on Corregidora's narrative by choosing not to follow the path trod by past generations of women. Unlike her ancestors, Ursa brings music to aid her in defining her moment of truth, a heroic moment of individual assertion characterized by her distinctive solo voice as part of the collective memory.

At first glance, the dual functions of cry-and-response seem disconnected. On the one hand, it signifies on the blues-based themes of jazz, as language swings off the pages through improvisatory riffs on female subjectivity; on the other hand, it "fingers the jagged grain" of a twentieth-century African American blues singer's life (Ellison, *Living with Music* 103). Yet these two streams of consciousness are related. In "Blues to Be Constitutional," music critic Stanley Crouch asserts that "because Afro-American culture is essentially oral, [it] is in danger of being dictated to by whoever has command of the microphone" (Crouch 159). Ursa's eventual command of the microphone, literally and metaphorically, like popular blues singers such as Ma Rainey and Bessie Smith, echoes "the sound and the repository of the nation's [new] myth" (160). Indeed, Ursa's voice emerges as a powerful instrument in much the same way as "women blues singers have become our cultural icons of sexual power" (Carby 480), liberating themselves and their audience through song.

Although *Corregidora* denotes Ursa's particular human experience on the foundation provided by the blues, which are rooted in the history and memory of the African American experience, the elements of jazz infused throughout the narrative inform Ursa's journey through language and characterize her achievement of individual assertion and ultimate freedom. *Corregidora* takes the form of what scholar Angelyn Mitchell describes as a "liberatory narrative" (Mitchell 4). Mitchell resituates the neoslave narrative within the context of twentieth-century African American women writers.

Mitchell defines the liberatory narrative as "a contemporary novel that engages the historical period of chattel slavery in order to provide new models of liberation by investigating the concept of freedom" (Mitchell 4). "Their primary function," continues Mitchell, "is in describing how to achieve freedom. In doing so the liberatory narrative seeks to eclipse the deterministic condition of racial enslavement" (4). Thus, the liberatory narrative ultimately frees not only the characters but also the readers through a "discussion of slavery as a *lieu de memoire* and by defamiliarizing slavery through illumination and interrogation" (150). *Corregidora* emancipates its readers by describing how a certain type of freedom and liberation can be obtained through the jazz aesthetic and stresses slavery by illuminating the residual effects of such a system on generations of Black women.

In Jones's novel, the melodic jazz riffs begin with the enslavement and oppression of the African American female body, but the text concludes on a different note, with Ursa finding agency through resistance. As bell hooks observes, "Oppressed people resist by identifying themselves as subjects, by defining their reality, shaping their new identity, naming their history, telling their story" (hooks 43). Ursa's final dialogue not only reconfigures her sexual relationship with Mutt but also transforms the act of bearing witness and making generations.

The novel itself is Ursa's addendum to the improvised slave narrative of Corregidora. The book provides us with a definition of freedom and portrays how the ideal can be obtained. For Ursa, freedom represents the ability to cry and respond to the narratives of her past and in the same breath to tell her own story, "somewhere behind the words" of the blues and within the nuances of jazz. Hence, if the story itself is an act of bearing witness and making generations, Ursa's final cry-and-response dialogue bears witness to the transformative aspect of making generations as she reconfigures the act in and through language. Ursa's final assertion advances her as a Wild Woman par excellence as she removes herself from the position of object and becomes the subject, the *I* within her final assertion. Ursa's final act is resistance as she transitions from the object of the blues to the subject of her own jazz fiction.

Chapter 3

THE JAZZ MOMENT

(Re)Envisioning Ralph Ellison's *Invisible Man* in Toni Morrison's *The Bluest Eye*

Improvisers, according to Paul Berliner in *Thinking in Jazz: The Infinite Art of Improvisation,* "perpetually make split-second decisions about suitable materials and their treatment" (Berliner 497). These decisions are rooted in memory, characterized by deliberate spontaneity, and replete with creative possibilities that transcend the musical score. How do authors create the moment of improvisation in writing? What linguistic signifiers allude to characters improvising in the moment? What is the process of improvisation? But first, how does a jazz novel improvise?

Toni Morrison's *The Bluest Eye* improvises on the "unsung" classic blues themes of the 1920s and 1930s. In the foreword to Paul Oliver's seminal text *Blues Fell This Morning,* Richard Wright "casts a bird's-eye view upon the meaning and implication of blues music" and cites three prominent themes or subjects that were omitted. Wright notes that in blues music: "the theme of spirituality, of other-worldliness is banned.... [T]hough constant reference is made to loved ones; little or no mention is made of the family as such.... [T]he locale of these songs shifts continuously and very seldom is a home site hymned or celebrated" (Wright xv).

Morrison's novel shatters the silence surrounding the themes of African American spirituality, family, and home life. *The Bluest Eye* interrogates the foundation of the African American family by confronting the dynamics of a home where the dark secret of father-daughter incest is put on display, portraying Pecola Breedlove's spiritual journey in search of agency and subjectivity. Although Ralph Ellison's *Invisible Man* was one of the first novels to introduce the taboo subject of father-daughter incest, Morrison places the issue at the forefront of her novel to illustrate its nuances within a deteriorating African American family.

The Bluest Eye tells the story of Pecola Breedlove's descent into madness. Morrison constructs a jazz-like narrative structure as she interweaves the voices of the community members through Pecola's story to show their complicity in her demise. Pecola's characterization as a mad Wild Woman at the end of the novel attests to the community's failure, and to a larger extent to the nation's inability, to nurture African American life.

Morrison lays out the blues as the foundational undertone of African American existence and examines the resistant, complex, and improvisational force of jazz as embodied in the character of Cholly Breedlove. Like Ursa Corregidor, Cholly can be read as a spectacle, a wild man of sorts, in that his past trauma precipitates his jazz moment of improvisation. Yet unlike Ursa, Cholly is not a performer or an artist and is thus devoid of a platform. Without a platform and an art form, Cholly's jazz moment is perverted: he uses his daughter as a platform, literally and figuratively, to achieve his individual moment of assertion. Morrison describes the jazz moment for the wild man as an ambiguous act of perversion, unyielding to reason, and surrounded by chaos. Rather than creating a heroic image—an improviser who writes his signature on the epidermis of life by leaving his mark[1]—she constructs Cholly as an antihero who tries and fails to gain power and agency through the rape of his daughter. This chapter takes interest in Cholly as a wild male figure and the relationship between Cholly's complexly ambiguous jazz moment of improvisation and the construction of Pecola as a mad Wild Woman. How does this moment of improvisation/violence become a destructive space, rendering the wild male improviser powerless?

The Trueblood episode in *Invisible Man* can serve as a lens to compare and contrast Cholly Breedlove's jazz moment of incestuous rape. Morrison constructs Cholly as a figure who represents jazz as defined by Ellison, and Cholly's jazz moment of improvisation is written into the narrative as a complex moment of sexual aggression that breaches the normative relationship between fathers and daughters and questions rather than grants power, identity, and agency.

The Bluest Eye seems a revision of Ellison's male-centered Trueblood episode. While both Trueblood and Cholly violate the incest taboo, the Trueblood episode fails to show the ramifications of such an act on the victim Matty Lou. Morrison remedies this silence by allowing Pecola to assert herself. In addition, Morrison pushes the boundaries of that episode beyond Ellison's marginalization of it through Trueblood's singular perspective. If Ellison depicts the shame inherent in Trueblood's tale, for Invisible Man as well as the larger community, Morrison reconstructs that shame into Claudia's feeling of guilt: she blames the community and the larger society for Pecola's circumstances. While Ellison relegates Trueblood's story to a fragment within the larger frame of Invisible Man's life, Morrison applies a magnifying lens to the episode and posits Pecola's story as the picture itself, framed by the community's denial and the nation's neglect. Yet Morrison's dialogue with or response to Ellison is not limited to the Trueblood episode. Morrison expounds on other parts of Ellison's narrative to describe a concise response to his silencing of the Black female experience. Understanding how the jazz lens works within the prologue to *Invisible Man* will help explain its significance in *The Bluest Eye*.

The prologue to *Invisible Man* introduces the three main components of the jazz lens: the Wild Woman figure, the jazz cry, and the jazz moment of improvisation. Ellison describes the process of transcendence as Invisible Man moves through various levels of sound and into the depths of the music. As Invisible Man listens to jazz trumpeter Louis Armstrong's "Black and Blue," he transcends his situation:

He not only entered the music but descended, like Dante, into its depths. And beneath the swiftness of the hot tempo there was a slower tempo and a cave and I entered it and looked around and heard an old woman singing a spiritual as full of Weltschmerz as flamenco, and beneath that lay a still lower level on which I saw a beautiful girl the color of ivory pleading in a voice like my mother's as she stood before a group of slave owners who bid for her naked body, and below that I found a lower level and a more rapid tempo. (*Invisible Man* 9)

This description subtly introduces the historical trajectory of African American music from "an old woman singing the spirituals" to "a lower level and a more rapid tempo"—that is, jazz. Invisible Man discovers improvisation in the language of a sermon filled with the jazz cry-and-response.

The subject of the sermon, "The Blackness of Black," is rooted in the blues, and jazz moments of improvisation weave in and out of the ritualized dialogue between preacher and audience. Similar to the dialogue found in Gayl Jones's *Corregidora*, the rhetoric of cry-and-response here depicts more than the obvious linguistic reciprocation between the congregants and the preacher.[2] Throughout the sermon, Ellison's visual line-by-line pacing of the cry-and-response dialogue sets the tempo, as his descriptive markers, *the cry* and *shout*, create a rhythm, underlining the cyclical pattern of communication between preacher and audience.

Both the visual pacing of language and the musically descriptive markers identify the sermon as more than the conventional call-and-response usually associated with the blues. The multiple voices used to create the cry-and-response dialogue involve language with double entendres and set forth the conditions of being Black: "black is and it aint, it will get you and it won't. Black will make you and un-make you" (*Invisible Man* 10). Being Black connotes both the literal and figurative sense. The rhetoric of the sermon encompasses the essence of the jazz ethos: the paradox of being Black as it relates to invisibility and hypervisibility, Black objectification in the face of white subjectivity.

Still within the lower level, Invisible Man encounters an old woman who attempts to define freedom, a theme shared by jazz and the novel. Like the sermon, the "old singer of spirituals" signifies on the jazz ethos through her story about killing her slave master, who is also the father of her sons. Like Ursa, the old woman transitions from object to subject. She begins as an object of slavery owned by her master whose survival depends on her acquiescence to his demands. Thus, she is a mere spectacle, an object of the master's gaze and desire. She exists for and because of her master and must resign herself to her situation. Though the old woman hates her master, "because I loved my sons I learned to love their father" (10).

Nevertheless, her love for her master does not overshadow her love for freedom. In fact, the idea of freedom as well as the inevitability that her sons will commit a more heinous crime of murder propels her to poison their father: "I loved him and give him the poison and he withered away like a frost-bit apple. Them boys woulda tore him to pieces with they homemade knives" (10). Although the old woman's ambivalence toward her master reveals blues sentiments, her use of poison as a murder weapon veers from the traditional blues tale scenario, which usually involves a knife.[3] Poison becomes an improvised and more subtle method of achieving the same end—the death of her master and thus her individual freedom. Here the Wild Woman is not only armed but stands outside the blues idiom that is central to her tale.

The question of freedom, which is fundamental here and throughout *Invisible Man*, signifies on the jazz aesthetic and is central to the old woman's narrative. Although freedom, like jazz, is difficult to denote, according to critic John Litweiler, the two go hand in hand: "The quest for freedom with a small f appears at the very beginning of jazz and reappears at every growing point in the music's history" (Litweiler 13). The cry-and-response dialogue about freedom reveals the jazz moment of improvisation, which follows a particular pattern: fragmentation, reconfiguration, and assertion/ultimate freedom. As I explain in the introduction, cry-and-response is a rhetorical trope that is subsumed under the master trope of call-and-response. The cry has something in it that says more than mere words can express "and it usually involves misinterpretation and ambiguity." The cry can be viewed as both articulate and inarticulate. Although the cry is usually surrounded by language, it is a musical signifier of inarticulacies; the meaning of the inarticulate cry stands outside of language. Some examples of inarticulate cries are characterized by silences, hard gazes, low crying, and screams.

When Invisible Man asks, "What is this freedom you love so well?" the old woman looked surprised, then thoughtful, then baffled. "I done forgot son. It's all mixed up. First I think it's one thing, then I think it's another. It gits my head spinning. I guess now it ain't nothing but knowing how to say what I got up in my head" (*Invisible Man* 11).

The old woman is caught off guard and feels a range of emotions from surprise to befuddlement. She begins her improvisatory answer through a fragmented state of mind: "It's all mixed up." She then collects her thoughts before concluding, "I guess now it ain't nothing but knowing how to say what I got up in my head" (11). Freedom thus forms within the moment of individual assertion. The ability to articulate what Ursa Corregidora calls one's "feeling ways" seems central to the notion of freedom. The old woman's ability to transcend the blues in a moment of assertion enables her to gain access to the freedom she loved enough to kill for and characterizes her as a jazz figure. The articulation of her final thought defines freedom and liberates her. As a figure of resistance, she arms herself with language.

The nameless narrator's quest for freedom reflects the freedom defined by the old Wild Woman. Unsatisfied with her answer and her digressions, he poses the question again, but this time a bit differently "But what about freedom?" This question of freedom, loosely defined as the ability to articulate/assert oneself, haunts Invisible Man and the other jazz-like characters that populate the narrative. The connections among music, orality, and freedom resound on the lower frequencies throughout the narrative from Invisible Man's first speech at the Battle Royal to his final magnum opus. Yet his initial encounter with jazz through Armstrong's incantations and the music's ability to enter him and move him to action mark him as a jazz figure.

Like Invisible Man, a similar "rapid tempo" in *The Bluest Eye* precedes Cholly Breedlove's entrance into the narrative and Pauline Breedlove's life: "Pauline was leaning idly on the fence. . . . [B]ehind her at some distance she heard whistling. One of these rapid, high-note riffs that black boys make up as they go while sweeping, shoveling, or just walking along. A kind of city-street music where laughter belies anxiety and joy is as short and straight as the blade of a pocketknife" (*Bluest Eye* 114). In this passage, Cholly's presence intertwines with jazz music, "a kind of city-street music." The music sounds informed by the blues tradition of laughing to keep from crying, as "laughter belies anxiety," and violence as described through the limited time span of joy and its relationship to the deadly blues weapon, the pocketknife. Cholly's music is rooted in the blues tradition yet is personal: he whistles his "own" music. The elements of jazz and blues music depicted in this scene historically relate to the transition from blues music to swing during this period.

The presence of jazz music as depicted in the whistle that catches Pauline's attention is characterized as both instrumental ("rapid, high-note riff") and improvisational ("something that black boys make up as they go"). Cholly's riffing marks him not only as an instrumentalist and improviser but also as a fragmented character. As scholar Krin Gabbard notes in *Jazz among the Discourses*, "the riff is a rhythmic melodic fragment, normally used repetitiously in answer to a lead melodic phrase or to another rhythmic fragment" (Gabbard 43). Cholly becomes the response to Pauline's cry for love and affection, "a simple Presence, an all embracing tenderness with strength and a promise of rest" (*Bluest Eye* 113). Pauline's fantasy encounter with this Presence, which she calls the "Stranger," is characterized by a "wordless" desire for understanding: "in none of her fantasies was she ever aggressive; she was usually idling by the riverbank, or gathering berries in a field when a someone appeared, with gentle and penetrating eyes, who—with no exchange of words—understood; and before whose glance her foot straightened and her eyes dropped. The someone had no face, no form, no voice, no odor" (113). The cry dwells outside of language, and the yearnings of Pauline's soul can only be articulated through music. Pauline is characterized throughout the text as a dreamer, marked by deformity, and she, like Morrison's Sula, can be read as an "artist without an art form" (*Sula* 121).

As a young woman, Pauline luxuriates in her solitude as she is left to care for the home. Pauline seems calmed and energized by the "stillness and isolation" of a quiet house, where she can "arrange and clean without interruption" (*Bluest Eye* 112). Yet at the age of fifteen, she tires of her role as housekeeper, as "fantasies about men and love and touching were drawing her mind and hands away from her work" (113). Pauline desires a "voiceless" encounter and can articulate herself only vicariously through Ivy, a member of the church choir. Morrison adopts specific lyrics from Ivy's rendition of "Take My Hand, Precious Lord," to express Pauline's sentiments and to inscribe her into the African American musical tradition:

When my life is almost gone
Hear my cry, hear my call
Hold my hand lest I fall
Take my hand, Precious Lord, Lead me on. (114)

Ivy sings of "the dark sweetness that Pauline could not name . . . of the Stranger who *knew*" (113). The insertion of this particular song suggests Pauline's identification with the music: Ivy held "in her mouth all of the sounds of Pauline's soul" (113). This tension between despair and hope suggests the blues tradition.

Our introduction to Cholly, which directly follows the lyrics, offers an intriguing juxtaposition, drawing our attention to a new music: "He came strutting right out of a Kentucky sun on the hottest day of the year . . . with his own music" (114). Cholly hears Pauline's cry and "with no exchange of words" responds with a telling gesture by "tickling her broken foot and kissing her leg" (115). This memory prefaces Cholly's jazz moment of improvisation, his rape of Pecola. This jazz scene serves as the catalyst for Cholly's act of incestuous violence.

Cholly's jazz moment takes place within the ambiguous realm of past memory conflated with present reality and follows the pattern of fragmentation, reconfiguration, and assertion. After the soloist is granted (temporary) freedom through his act of assertion, the moment fades, and he becomes conscious of his actions within the present reality. Although both Trueblood and Cholly improvise within a moment of incestuous violence, they are distinguished by the decisions they make after their respective transgressions.

In *Invisible Man*, the "well liked" Jim Trueblood is a sharecropper "who told the old stories with a sense of humor and a magic that made them come alive" (*Invisible Man* 46). Yet once the surrounding community, the "folks" at the school, find out he committed the vile act of incest and would permit his daughter, Matty Lou, to "birth his abomination," he is considered a disgrace and a pariah (46). Trueblood's story of incest "had caused quite a bit of outrage up at the school, and now his name was never mentioned above a whisper" (46). In fact, the "biggity school folks" try to force him out of town (52). According to Trueblood, "They offered to send us clean outta the county, pay our way and everything and give me a hundred dollars to git settled with. But we likes it here so I told 'em NO. Then they sent a fellow out here, a big fellow too, and he said if I didn't leave they was going to turn the white folks loose on me. . . . I found they was tryin' to get rid of us 'cause they said we was a disgrace" (52). Instead of attempting to rehabilitate the family, the community decides to cover up the secret of incest by removing the evidence—the family itself. But Trueblood declines, instead choosing to expose the secret in exchange for money and/or goods.

Jim Trueblood is characterized as a master storyteller. Relating the incident to Mr. Norton, Trueblood "cleared his throat, his eyes gleaming and his voice taking on a deep, incantatory quality, as though he had told the story many, many times" (53). Patronized by white members of the community, Jim uses the story and his storytelling skills to earn a living: "'For they heard 'bout what happened to us out here I couldn't git no help from nobody. Now lotta folks is curious and goes outta they way to help" (53). Echoing the historical commodification of the African American female body in slavery, Matty Lou's body is conquered—in this case, by an African American man (her father)—and the story is told to a white audience in exchange for goods.

Here, Black pathology becomes commodified: As Trueblood says: "I went to see the white folks then and they gave me help. That's what I don't understand. I done the worse thing a man could ever do in his family and instead of chasin' me out of the country they gimme more help than they ever give any other colored man, no matter how good a nigguh he was. . . . I'm better off than I've ever been before" (67). Even Trueblood cannot understand how or why he is benefiting from doing "the worse thing a man could ever do." Yet because he is making a profit, he continues to tell his narrative of incest to any passerby who will listen. Like the other whites, Mr. Norton compensates Trueblood, giving him one hundred dollars.

Trueblood's narrative of what happened the night he impregnated his daughter is told through his perspective and in his own voice. The perspectives and voices of both Matty Lou and Kate are heard only through his voice, thus muffling the female victims. In effect, Trueblood not only narrates their story, but also interprets Matty Lou's (re)actions:

Matty Lou can't hold out no longer and gits to movin' herself. First she was tryin' to push me away and I'm tryin' to hold her down to keep from sinnin'. Then I'm pullin' away and shushin' her to be quiet so's not to wake her Ma, when she grabs holt to me and holds tight. She didn't want me to go then—and to tell the honest-to-God truth I found out that I didn't want to go neither. . . . [T]he more wrigglin' and twistin' we don tryin' to git away, the more we wanted to stay. (60)

Trueblood's narrative detail can be interpreted in various ways; however, making Matty Lou a participant rather than a victim seems to appease his guilt and transforms the incestuous act from an act of rape to one of consent. Because her side of the story is muted, readers will never know why or if Matty Lou actually began to move or held tight. In contrast, Morrison's telling narrative positions readers as outsiders; unlike Matty Lou, Pecola is not silenced.[4]

Morrison begins *The Bluest Eye* with "Quiet as it's kept" (1) to suggest the opposite—we are entering into a pseudo-private tale. Morrison's contradictory beginning reveals that the novel's secret is actually common knowledge and not so quietly kept. Morrison brings the issue of father-daughter incest to the fore by focusing on the moment of incestuous rape and contextualizing that moment within a larger frame that holds the family, community, and music accountable for Pecola's fate. The unkept secret, according to narrator Claudia MacTeer, concerns Pecola Breedlove and the stifled marigolds that never bloomed. Claudia and her sister, Frieda, planted the flowers as a symbolic gesture to ensure the safe delivery of Pecola's baby, but the marigolds failed to blossom, and for Claudia and Frieda, "what is clear now is that of all of that hope, fear, lust, love, and grief, nothing remains but Pecola and the unyielding earth. Cholly Breedlove is dead; our innocence too. The seeds shriveled and died; her baby too" (*Bluest Eye* 9). Unlike Trueblood's story, Cholly Breedlove's narrative of incest is related not in his own voice but from the perspective of an omniscient narrator. Whereas Trueblood describes his actions through his own limited perspective and (mis)understands his dream, the omniscient narrator reports on Cholly's trauma-filled past and attempts to contextualize his thoughts and empathize with if not justify his actions. The rape of Pecola becomes contextualized within Cholly's blues-ridden existence.

The blues ethos weaves into the first sentence of Cholly's narrative, positing him as a character who is born into the blues: "When Cholly was four days old, his mother wrapped him in two blankets and one newspaper and placed him on a junk heap by the railroad" (65). The link between the blues and the railroad is significant to the history of migration that characterizes the African American experience. According to scholar Farah Jasmine Griffin, "The railroad, long a symbol of freedom in the African-American oral tradition, reappears in the northbound blues. By invoking it, the blues lyricist calls upon an image packed with cultural significance for his audience" (*"Who Set You Flowin'?"* 19). Morrison's invocation of the railroad is twofold, with different meanings for Cholly and his mother.

According to scholar Hazel Carby, "The train, which had symbolized freedom and mobility for men in male blues songs[, for women signified] a mournful signal of imminent desertion and future loneliness" (Carby 19). By placing both Cholly and his mother in the first sentence of the narrative of Cholly's life, Morrison positions him at the crossroads of both freedom and "future loneliness." However, Aunt Jimmy rescues Cholly and raises and cares for him until her death. At this point, Cholly's tale of desertion and freedom begins to unfold.

Understanding Cholly's search for and ultimate denial of freedom within the jazz moment of improvisation requires first analyzing his relationship to freedom. As a child, Cholly is unaware of the full ramifications of Aunt Jimmy's death—that he is without guardianship and therefore is free to do as he pleases. His reaction to Aunt Jimmy's body and to the funeral shifts from little understanding to recognition. During and after the funeral, Cholly basks in the attention directed at him "as a member of the family, one of the bereaved" (*Bluest Eye* 111). The attention means that Cholly is not aware of how Aunt Jimmy's death will ultimately affect his life:

> Cholly had not yet fully realized his aunt was dead. Everything was so interesting. Even at the graveyard he felt nothing but curiosity, and when his turn had come to view the body at the church, he had put his hand out to touch the corpse to see if it

were really ice cold like everybody said. But he drew his hand back quickly. Aunt Jimmy looked so private, and it seemed wrong somehow to disturb that privacy. He had trudged back to his pew dry-eyed amid tearful shrieks and shouts of others, wondering if he should try to cry. (113)

Aunt Jimmy's cold body poses an obstacle between her and Cholly. Death becomes the barrier between living and freedom. Only after Aunt Jimmy's death does Cholly realize that no one is responsible for him or how he chooses to live his life—in essence, he is free. His recognition of this freedom occurs when he is out in the field with Darlene. When Darlene comments on her fear that a stain on her dress will result in a whipping by her mother, Cholly becomes aware that "Aunt Jimmy was dead, for he missed the fear of being whipped" (116). Although Cholly's freedom is born in this moment of recognition, his sense of that freedom is checked by the reality that the absence of a loving guardian's reprimand does not guarantee the absence of social apparatuses outside of his control, such as racism.

Cholly's freedom to engage in sexual intercourse without recourse is stifled both figuratively and literally as he is caught by two white men. Out in the woods, he and Darlene begin to experiment sexually, first with kissing and touching and finally with intercourse. Because it is Cholly's first time, he is nervous and afraid yet intrigued by the prospect of this particular rite of passage:

Cholly dropped his pants down to his knees. Their bodies began to make sense to him, and it was not as difficult as he had thought it would be. She moaned a little, but the excitement collecting inside him made him close his eyes and regard her moans as no more than pine sighs over his head. Just as he felt an explosion threaten, Darlene froze and cried out. He thought he had hurt her, but when he looked at her face, she was staring wildly at something over his shoulder. He jerked around. There stood two white men. (116)

The white men in the woods emasculate Cholly and undermine his only instrument of freedom, his phallus. The phallus, a symbol of male agency, is nullified by the white man's artillery. As Cholly faces the barrel of the white man's gun, he is again confronted by death, the barrier between life and freedom. Cholly chooses life by adhering to the demands of the two white men and continues his sexual interlude with Darlene. Because he is no longer able to function sexually, Cholly suffers an internal and symbolic death by means of his emasculation: "the flashlight man lifted his gun down from his shoulder, and Cholly heard the clop of metal. He dropped back to his knees.... With a violence born of total helplessness, he pulled her dress up, lowered his trousers and underwear.... Darlene put her hands over her face as Cholly began to simulate what had gone on before. He could do no more than make-believe" (117).

The flashlight can be seen as a symbol of the white man's phallus as it illuminates the white man's gun, a symbol of the white man's strong armor. In addition, the flashlight "wormed its way into [Cholly's] guts and turned the sweet taste of muscadine into rotten fetid bile" (117). Turning what began as a sweet sexual encounter into a rotten exposition of his helplessness, the white men invert the sexual rite of passage, changing it into a racialized rite of passage that exposes Cholly's low position within the social hierarchy.

Cholly's sense of freedom or unfreedom connects to sexual virility. The recognition of his freedom as a man ties to his sexual rite of passage, which is never fully realized. Because Cholly is helpless and not free to retaliate by venting his hatred for the white men, he makes Darlene the object of his hatred:

> Never did he once consider directing his hatred toward the hunters. Such an emotion would have destroyed him. They were big, white, armed men. He was small, black, and helpless. His subconscious knew what his conscious mind did not guess—that hating them would have consumed him, burned him up like a piece of soft coal, leaving only flakes of ash and a question mark of smoke. He was, in time, to discover that hatred of white men—but not now. Not in impotence but later, when the hatred could find sweet expression. For now, he hated the one who had created the situation, the one who bore witness to his failure, his impotence. The one person he had

not been able to protect, to spare, and to cover from the round moon glow of the flashlight. (119)

The description of Cholly as small and Black directly contrasts to the primer that begins his narrative: "seefatherheisbigandstrong" (3). Here, Cholly as a "small, black, helpless" child is no match for the "big, white, armed men." This paragraph not only describes his feelings for Darlene but also serves as the blueprint for his feelings toward all the women he will encounter in his life, including his own daughter. Although his castration is put in sexual terms, as the white man's gun sullies his sense of virility, it is further reinscribed when he travels to Macon in search of his father and is twice abandoned. Thus, being born into the blues was only the beginning for Cholly. The culmination of the events of his life—his objectification by two white hunters, his father's denial of his existence, and the death of the only person who cared for him—is articulated in the jazz moment of improvisation, his rape of Pecola. Although the events of Cholly's life make it possible to view him through a blues lens, his final act of rape inscribes him as a jazz figure.

Music critic Albert Murray asserts that the blues idiom lyric is a statement about the facts of life: "Not unlike ancient tragedy, it would have the people for whom it is composed and performed confront, acknowledge, and proceed in spite of and even in terms of the ugliness and meanness inherent in the human condition. It is thus a device for making the best of a bad situation" (*The Hero and the Blues* 36). Trueblood's lyrical tale of incest is marked by and is characteristic of the blues idiom. After Kate and the community confront and scorn him, Trueblood decides to leave his house and think about his current situation. He composes his own blues idiom lyric by improvising on a church song: "Finally one night, way early in the mornin', I looks up and sees the stars and I starts singin'. I don't mean to, I didn't think 'bout it, just start singin'. All I know is I ends up singin' the blues" (*Invisible Man* 66). While singing his improvised lyric, Trueblood confronts the facts of life, acknowledges his current circumstance, and finally decides to go home and proceed in spite of the ugliness of his actions: "While I'm singing them blues I makes up my mind that I ain't nobody but myself and ain't nothing I can do but let whatever is gonna happen happen. I made up my mind that I was goin back home and face Kate; yeah, and face Matty Lou too" (66). Trueblood's insistence on taking responsibility for his actions and living in spite of the blues distinguishes him from Cholly.

Cholly's inability to confront or acknowledge the ugliness of his actions prevents him from taking responsibility for the damage he causes Pecola. Although both Trueblood and Cholly experience the jazz moment within a moment of sexual violence, Trueblood remains within the blues idiom as a consequence of his determination to return to his family and resign himself to his circumstance. Cholly's experience seems to connote the dangerous spirit of jazz, which gives him license to be dangerously free, and thus he transcends the blues within the jazz moment of improvisation.[5]

Characterized by a pattern of fragmentation, reconfiguration, and assertion, the jazz moment is ultimately a moment of improvisation—sudden, unexpected, yet calculated, as if the jazz figure experiencing the moment has prepared for it all throughout his/her life. It is a psychological moment of otherworldliness, as past memories are yoked to present realities. It is also a moment of self-assertion, as characters define themselves and their identities in an attempt to achieve ultimate freedom. At this time, the historical past replays in the mind of the character and presents memories as fragments. The protagonist reconfigures these memories into the reality of the moment and improvises within that moment. The improvisational moment involves assertion, taking place in the break between memory and present reality. Not until the act is complete does the protagonist regain a sense of reality and choose whether to fight with life or flee.

In the jazz moment of improvisation, Cholly is characterized as a fragmented jazz figure:

The pieces of Cholly's life could become coherent only in the head of a musician. Only those who talk their talk through the gold of curved metal, or in the touch of black-and-white rectangles and taut skins and strings echoing from wooden corridors, could give true form to his life. Only they would know how to connect the heart of a red watermelon to the asafetida bag to the muscadine to the flashlight on his behind to the fists of money to the lemonade in a Mason jar to a man called Blue and come up with what all of that meant in joy, in pain, in anger, in love, and give it its final and pervading ache of freedom. Only a musician would sense, know, without even knowing that he knew, that Cholly was free. (*Bluest Eye* 159)

The insertion of instrumentation to convey the means by which a musician could communicate the fragmentary pieces of Cholly's life and deem him whole signifies on jazz music. Because the pieces of Cholly's life are fragmented and unable to be connected in a way that makes linguistic sense, he seems figuratively broken. The musician's ability to connect Cholly's traumatic past to his present emotional state creates a free form that characterizes him as a jazz figure.

Cholly's life includes various episodes of trauma and emotional baggage that he must piece together so that he can improvise. Doing so enables Cholly to create, within the jazz moment, a foundation for improvisation and ultimate freedom. Cholly is characterized as having experienced everything and as now having no interest in anything or anyone but himself: "he was free to live his fantasies, and free even to die, the how and the when of which held no interest for him. In those days, Cholly was truly free. Abandoned in a junk heap by his mother, rejected for a crap game by his father, there was nothing more to lose. He was alone with his own perceptions and appetites, and they alone interested him" (126). Cholly's self-interest, paired with his traumatic past, aids in creating his solo in the break. In *Corregidora*, the break happens within dialogue; in *The Bluest Eye*, the opposite occurs. Cholly's break takes place in a moment of incoherence and inarticulacy. Morrison reveals the perverted moment of individual assertion through Cholly's drunken state of inarticulacy: "Only in drink was there some break, some floodlight, and when that closed, there was oblivion" (126).

The first sentence leading to Cholly's solo, his rape of his daughter, begins with Cholly "stagger[ing] home reeling drunk and [seeing] his daughter in the Kitchen" (127). Morrison describes Pecola not by name but as "his daughter," placing her in a subordinate position and constructing a very obvious power dynamic. Moreover, Pecola is also virtually invisible: "Cholly saw her dimly and could not tell

ELLISON'S *INVISIBLE MAN* IN MORRISON'S *THE BLUEST EYE*   63

what he saw or what he felt" (161). Cholly's reaction, "revulsion, guilt, pity, then love," as "guilt and impotence rose in a bilious duet," results from Pecola's helpless presence and what he sees as an object that represents his failure as a father. Cholly confronts and acknowledges the fact that he cannot do anything for her or give her the love that she deserves. His guilt, impotence, and past abandonment by both parents render him incapable of supplying Pecola with the love that she needs. Although Cholly understands the facts of his life, unlike Trueblood he does not try to make the best of a bad situation. Instead, Cholly falters in the break and reconfigures the object of his guilt and impotence as the object of his affection.

Both Trueblood and Cholly are in dreamlike states when the rapes occur. They transpose the visual unreality to the practical reality. Trueblood does this through his dream, while Cholly does so through a flashback to Pauline. As Cholly watches Pecola wash dishes, his present reality collides with his memory of the past, and his daughter becomes his wife with a single "quiet and pitiful gesture":

> Her hands were going around and around a frying pan, scraping flecks of black into cold, greasy dishwater. The timid, tucked-in look of the scratching toe—that was what Pauline was doing the first time he saw her in Kentucky. . . . A desire to cover her foot with his hand and gently nibble away the itch from the calf with his teeth. He did it then, and started Pauline into laughter. He did it now. (128)

Cholly's flashback creates a mental illusion; paired with his drunkenness, it puts him into an otherworldly state of mind. He is cast in animalistic terms as he crawls on "all fours toward" Pecola (128). Cholly feels a mixture of emotions: "The confused mixture of his memories of Pauline and the doing of a wild forbidden thing excited him, and a bolt of desire ran down his genitals, giving it length, and softening the lips of his anus. Surrounding all of this lust was a border of politeness. He wanted to fuck her—tenderly" (128). Psychologically, Cholly has transposed his feelings of lust for Pauline to Pecola. Like Matty Lou, Pecola is silenced, and what is heard is not articulate. Only after the rape is Cholly conscious of Pecola: "Following the disintegration—the falling away—of sexual desire, he was conscious of her wet, soapy hands on his wrists, the fingers clenching, but whether her grip was from a hopeless but stubborn struggle to be free, or from some other emotion, he could not tell" (128).

The falling away of sexual desire can also be viewed as Cholly's fall from grace. Pecola's grip, much like Matty Lou's, is ambiguous, yet it brings Cholly back to reality. Her struggle to be free is juxtaposed with his dangerously free attitude. The reality of his action is so painful that he leaves her lying, passed out, on the floor (129). The moment of sexual violence is filled with improvisation and assertion. Here, improvisation appears as a sudden response to fill the void that characterizes Pecola's life. For Cholly, improvisation is a method of creation. As his impotence is remedied, his phallus becomes the agent with which he articulates his emotions. Cholly is devoid of a platform for creation, so Pecola becomes his canvas.

Reading *The Bluest Eye* through a jazz lens enables us to view the jazz moment of improvisation as a moment of sexual violence that transgresses societal norms and offers a new way of reading the moment of individual assertion as involving powerlessness as well as endangerment. Morrison depicts the community through the social organization of jazz and uses ambiguity as well as a play on language to depict the ambiguous nature of the soloist and his precarious position as he strives to obtain freedom and power through individual assertion.

Morrison questions the costs at which the powerless obtain power. Cholly's moment of improvisation constitutes his only moment of individual assertion and in effect gives him the illusion of power; but it also silences and ultimately denies Pecola a voice, as she passes out. As the soloist asserts himself, he in effect denies the other group members power and agency. Thus, the heroic image can exist only at the expense of others.

Jazz explains Cholly's impulse to violence. This same impulse to violence can be related to Invisible Man's assertion that "this music demanded action." And the kind of action the music demanded seeps into Invisible Man's speeches and leads to violence on various occasions. For Trueblood, a different kind of music led to an adverse reaction. Trueblood sings the blues, which leads to a nonviolent reaction. Although his act is taboo, his choice to return and deal with his blues remains true to blues tradition. When jazz is involved, the reaction is resistance and the result is violence.

That Morrison would explain Cholly through the lens of jazz speaks volumes: his inability to articulate himself verbally leads to the physical violence against Pecola. Cholly's inability to articulate his transgression couples with his struggle for the right emotion. Thus, his action is countered by an oppositional effect: he fucks her tenderly. Cholly's mix of emotion remains suspended during the brief moment of rape, and we are left with a sense that the act was supposed to instill a sense of power. Some readers might even begin to sympathize with Cholly's character, as Morrison's depiction of his previous traumas leaves him in the position of victim rather than victimizer. However, Pecola's ritualized dialogue at the end of the text troubles our view of Cholly, as we learn that he has raped her on at least one other occasion.

Pecola's cry-and-response dialogue indicates not only her descent into madness but the effects of disillusionment on children of the 1970s Black Is Beautiful movement. It also reveals the community's inability to support and uphold some of its most vulnerable members, Black girls. With Pecola, Morrison introduces a variegated form of wildness, one that is predicated on the effects of racism, on the imposition of standards of white beauty on a Black child, and on the dissolution of the Black family by means of the Black male.

Written in the 1970s and set in the 1940s, *The Bluest Eye* not only serves as a response to Ellison but can also be read as an answer to the 1965 Moynihan Report, which outlined the dissolution of the Black family through a survey of the poorest populations in America. The report, written by Daniel Patrick Moynihan, an assistant secretary of labor under President Lyndon Johnson and later a US senator, came under criticism for blaming Black women for the deterioration, dissolution, and future fate of the Black family. Morrison's novel reclaims the female figure and repositions her as only part of rather than the entirety of the problem. If anything, Morrison takes the Black male to task not only for perpetuating the dissolution of the Black family, which began with American ideals rooted in racist ideology, but for adding insult to injury by abdicating his responsibility to the family. Unlike Trueblood, who uses blues ideology to return to his home and do the right thing, Morrison posits jazz's liberatory ideology as dangerous when the Black male uses it not only for violent action but as a license for freedom.

Freedom provides the underlying rhythm of Morrison's lyrical jazz novel. According to Duke Ellington, "Jazz is a good barometer of freedom. . . . [T]he music is so free that many people say it is the only unhampered, unhindered expression of complete freedom yet produced in this country" (qtd. in M. Tucker 295). The jazz moment is both a moment of freedom and a moment of improvisation for Cholly. He creates chaos out of order, and his actions are unhindered and unhampered for the first time in his life. Musician John Corbett describes improvisation as "a compromise between order and disorder . . . a negotiation between codes and their pleasurable dismantling" (qtd. in Gabbard 237). This definition not only describes the process of improvisation in jazz music but also applies to how improvisation works in the jazz text. As characters use improvisation to achieve freedom, they are in effect negotiating compliance with societal codes and choosing to resist those codes.

Cholly dismantles the incest code in a moment of resistance, a violation that not only underscores the jazz moment of improvisation but reveals a reality endured by many young African American women. Unable to answer the difficult question of why father-daughter incest occurs, Morrison advises readers to seek refuge in how incest happens, which is ultimately a question of process. That process is cloaked in the rapid tempo of jazz and found in a moment of dangerous freedom in which the victimizer is the improviser who defies traditional moral codes despite the consequences, and the victim is the sheet music, unacknowledged, unaccounted for, yet still being played.

Chapter 4

WILD WOMEN DON'T HAVE THE BLUES

Improvising Women in Toni Morrison's
Jazz and Ann Petry's *The Street*

In Toni Morrison's *Jazz*, we enter the predominantly male discourse that surrounds jazz through the lens of a female narrator, who introduces us to a community of Wild Women. The narrator uses improvisation, repetition, and anticipation as she records the central tale of the narrative, the murder of Dorcas Manfred by Joe Trace. Through various narrative voices we discover the events leading up to Joe's crime within his jazz moment of improvisation and the aftermath of his choices. Here the jazz moment occurs within a moment of intimate violence that leads to individual assertion. Yet Joe's heinous act robs him of agency, renders him powerless, and transposes all that he loses to Dorcas.

The moment does not belong to Joe, but instead provides a temporary moment of power for the victim as opposed to the victimizer. In this moment, we hear Dorcas's voice through her loud silence as she refuses to name her killer. Dorcas is written into the narrative as a figure of resistance due to her silence, yet her story is mired and intertwined with that of the armed Wild Woman in the narrative: Violet, who "was practically all anybody talked about when they talked about Dorcas' death" (*Jazz* 75). The narrator weaves her voice throughout the narrative breaks of each character's solo perspective and offers improvised insights into the lives of the people in the community.

Through Joe's murder of Dorcas, the narrator traces Joe's ancestry back to his mother Wild, and we learn of his unmistakable connection to her. Morrison's narrative draws attention to the complex typography of Wild Women as primitive, licentious, armed divas. What makes *Jazz* so significant is Morrison's depiction of armed Wild Women during the late 1920s. According to the narrator, "All over the country black women were armed" (74). The armed Wild Woman as subject transitions from the primitive spectacle, as seen through the characterization of Joe's mother, Wild, and sits outside of the youthful boundaries that border the irresistible licentious diva, as portrayed in Dorcas. Although these women share a common bond in Joe Trace, Violet champions the spirit of jazz and is one of the last Wild Women standing.

This chapter explores the evolution of the Wild Woman as she is historically constructed as a primitive spectacle, honored within the blues as a sexually liberated subject, and depicted in twentieth-century African American literary texts as dangerously armed. *Jazz* connects the multifaceted construction of the Wild Woman to music and violence. Morrison experiments with the trope of the Wild Woman, depicting her in all of her diversity as she extends and revises her image and significance within African American culture and specifically jazz discourse. With its narrative metaphors, predominantly female perspectives, and cacophonous meditation on the violence inherent in the music and the consequences of that violence for African American women, *Jazz* seems primarily concerned with depicting the possibilities the music presented for Black women as they appropriated the discourse and pursued entrance into the art form.

Ida Cox is responsible for writing the term *Wild Woman* into the classic blues tradition. Cox, the Uncrowned Queen of the Blues, initially gained fame as a blues singer in the 1920s and 1930s and is best known for her signature song, "Wild Women Don't Have the Blues" (1924), which produced the image of the archetypal Wild Woman during the classic blues period. Cox left the spotlight during the 1940s, leading to speculation that she had died; however, she had actually retreated to Knoxville, Tennessee, to search for God. Her symbolic rebirth occurred in 1961, when she agreed to record an album with Coleman Hawkins. The release of *Blues for Rampart Street*, made Cox one of the first Wild Women reincarnated into the jazz tradition.[1]

In *Blues Legacies and Black Feminism*, Angela Davis notes, "Ida Cox's 'Wild Women Don't Have the Blues' became the most famous portrait of the nonconforming, independent woman, and her 'Wild Woman' has become virtually synonymous with the blues queen herself" (38). Davis includes Bessie Smith and Gertrude "Ma" Rainey among the blues singers who were Wild Women and boldly explored that theme in their music. According to Davis, the Wild Woman "consciously rejects mainstream values, especially those prescribing passivity in relations with men" (38). Cox's hit song describes the Wild Woman as powerful, fearless, and independent due to her command of her mind, emotions, and body.

"Wild Women Don't Have the Blues" delineates a telltale blues that reveals a counterhegemonic feminist discourse about intimate male-female relationships. The song constructs a dichotomy between the traditional blues-ridden female and the worry-free, nonconventional, antiblues subject—the Wild Woman. Unlike the blues women "who sit around all day and moan / wondering why their wandering papas don't come home," Wild Women show no such concern: "wild women don't worry, wild women don't have no blues." Read through a feminist lens, the lyrics reconfigure the phallocentric intimate male-female relationship model into a female-centered discourse. Indeed, like the "wandering papas" of these blues women, Wild Women are at liberty to "get full of liquor" and "walk the streets all night," only to "come home and put [their men] out if [they] don't act right."

Cox admonishes the blues woman to forget about being an "angel" and instead, "get real wild." Here, the term *wild* is, among other things, a signifier for licentious behavior. Wild women are instructed to "never be on the square / 'Cause if you do he'll have a woman everywhere." A woman would take back a man's only power over her—phallic power—as she preempts the inevitable (him leaving, lying, or cheating) by closing herself off emotionally and physically. Emotionally secure, sexually liberated, and characteristically independent, Wild Women do not have the blues because they do not subscribe to the stereotypical roles that have defined how women should act within the confines of a relationship.

Although the song evinces an antiblues sentiment, it is rooted in the blues tradition. Thus Wild Women are part and parcel of the blues idiom they resist. This resistance of the blues ethos within the classic blues tradition seems to empower the Wild Woman. Due to her central position, she feels free enough to criticize the institution that has aided in her construction. Empowerment enables her to rebuke the blues tradition by creating a space for herself. In addition to being a popular classic blues theme and figure, the Wild Woman image recurs in African American jazz narratives, but has received little if any attention within the jazz literary tradition.

Scholar Jurgen Grandt concludes that the connections among jazz, (political) power, and violence are a theme that appears in a myriad of jazz texts, including in Sidney Bechet's *Treat It Gentle*, Morrison's *Jazz*, Ann Petry's "Solo on the Drums," "Marie of the Cabin Club," and *The Street*. Moreover, continues Grandt,

> The suggestion [that there is more than a casual connection between jazz and violence] deepens when we remember Langston Hughes's description of drowning out the sound of exploding artillery shells in besieged Madrid by playing his Ellington, Goodman, or Lunceford records at full volume . . . ; of Ralph Ellison's Invisible man, who plays Armstrong's recording of "What Did I Do to Be So Black and Blue" as a prelude to the battle royal . . . ; or of Amiri Baraka's Clay [in *Dutchman and the Slave*], who is fatally stabbed after he exclaims that Charlie Parker would have roamed the streets of New York city murdering white people had he not had a saxophone. (Grandt 44)

However, Grandt's analysis misses the central impetus of the violence: the Wild Women in these jazz texts. If we take gender into account, we notice that in *Treat It Gentle*, Omar's struggle is worthwhile only because of Marie, whom he compares to a "wild bird" (Bechet 11). In "Solo on the Drums," Kid Jones's fantasy of dismembering his rival bandmate is prompted due to his Wild Woman, who decides to leave him for another man. Lutie's nightmare and subsequent violent killing of Boots in *The Street* results in part from her Wild Woman status; and all the bizarre violent acts in *Jazz* can be attributed to the novel's Wild Women. Further, Invisible Man plays Armstrong's recording not only as a prelude to the battle royal but also as a preface to the wild old woman who poisons (instead of knifing) her master, and Baraka's Clay is murdered by a wild white woman only moments after remarking that if Bessie Smith, the archetypal Wild Woman, "had killed some white people she wouldn't have needed that music" (*Dutchman* 35). At the center of the jazz text, where music and violence meet, is the Wild Woman of the jazz tradition and her unmistakable quest for power and agency.

The relationship among improvisation, violence, and the Wild Woman in African American literary texts and more specifically the jazz narrative leads to the following questions: How is the Wild Woman appropriated throughout African American literature? How does the Wild Woman achieve power and agency through improvisation? How does the evolution of the Wild Woman in literature figure in the discourse of Black female resistance?

The literary evolution of the African American Wild Woman from sexual object to improvising subject began in 1852 with Harriet Beecher Stowe's *Uncle Tom's Cabin* and continued through the 1992 publication of *Jazz*. The reconfiguration of the Wild Woman seems particularly explicit not only in *Jazz* but also in *The Street* (1946). Both Morrison and Petry deconstruct the image of the Wild Woman by exploring prior layers of meaning and signification attributed to her. Both books are uniquely complex in their depiction of Wild Women who resist society's definitions of morality and redefine what it means to be wild—without regulation or control.

Although much has been written about jazz improvisation from the perspective of ethnomusicologists, many of whom romanticize it and praise improvisers for their enlightening and innovative riffs, little has been written about moments of improvisation in fiction and even less about Black female improvisers. To analyze the darker side of improvisation—improvisation as a form of deviance and as an intermediary to acts of violence performed by Wild Women—this chapter explores moments of violence and disorder in jazz fiction and how the Wild Black woman negotiates identity, agency, and power. How do these moments of violence in the jazz text aid in the (re)construction of the African American Wild Woman by countering the theory of a "demoralized" Black female identity?

Scholar Kimberly Wallace asserts that "the bodies of black women have not only been identified as erotic objects but have symbolized the most extreme sexuality imaginable: wild, insatiable, and deviant."

Historically, the term *Wild Woman* has been synonymous with such terms as *out of control, untamed, licentious, wicked, alluring,* and *overtly sexual,* among others. The connection between the Black female body and "wild" sexuality has roots that extend deep into the 1800s. According to scholar Maria Cristina Nisco:

> Saartjie Baartman, known to the Western audience as the Hottentot Venus, can be said to fully embody darkness for her being both African and a woman. Her black body was a mystery to the white European gaze, which consequently caged it and turned it into a mere object of curiosity and knowledge: the excessiveness of her genitals and buttocks were shown as a proof of the wild sexuality characterizing black women. Parts of her body were exhibited during her life as well as her death (the Musée de l'Homme in Paris kept them until 1992). (65)[2]

The link between the Black female body and wild sex and sexuality has subsequently reappeared as a theme in both African American literature and music. Although blues music seems to connect the idea of independence, willfulness, sex, and sexuality to the wild African American woman, such has not always been the case in literature. In twentieth-century American literature, before there was a Wild Woman, there was a wild child.

Uncle Tom's Cabin contains one of the first references to the African American female as wild and unruly—a slave child, Topsy. Stowe's novel, known for its stereotypical depictions of African Americans, aided in the proliferation of the trope of the African American female wild child who is motherless, inarticulate, and in need of reform. Scholar Jim O'Laughlin notes: "the wild child, separated from her mother and mistreated, was a familiar trope in sentimental fiction. In fact, Stowe's solution for the problem of a wild child, the love of a substitute mother, was by no means unusual" (581). Further, O'Laughlin argues that the shift in the character portrayal of Topsy occurred with the (re)articulation of Topsy "by readers, adapters, and even those politically hostile to Stowe . . . in other novels, plays, poems, songs, advertisements, newspaper reports, letters to the editor, etc." (581). O'Laughlin cites George Aiken's theatrical adaptation of the novel as a source of one of the first re-creations of the character typology of Topsy (581). With Topsy's transformation into Broadway persona came the complexities associated with the African American female image exuding a form of sexuality. Unlike Stowe's novel, which ends with Topsy's freedom, the theatrical adaptation reimprisons the Black female body in the gaze of the white dominant figure, thus moving Topsy from sentimental subject to sexualized object. Aiken adds the character of Gumption Cute, who propositions Topsy: "Topsy, you can make my fortune, and your own, too. I've an idee in my head that is worth a million of dollars. . . . Well, as I was saying, Barnum made his money by exhibiting a woolly horse; now wouldn't it be an all-fired speculation to show you as the woolly gal?" (O'Laughlin 582). Cute offers to make a "sight" of Topsy and allow her to keep a portion of the proceeds, clearly viewing her as a sexualized and commodified object. Cute produces a different kind of Wild Child dynamic by constructing a complex ideological space that reaffirms the idea of the Black female body as spectacle and commodity. Topsy thus becomes a descendant of Baartman's African American Wild Woman tradition. Yet Topsy's refusal to go along with Cute's plan also marks her as a figure of resistance.

If Topsy is the quintessential Wild Child of the South, Frado, in Harriet Wilson's *Our Nig*, can be read as the mirror image in the North. Scholar Carla Peterson explains, "Like Stowe's Topsy, [Frado] is depicted as a 'wild, frolicky thing' whom white readers might well have viewed with condescending mockery rather than identification, but in whom black readers might well have recognized a figure of resistance." Further, according to Peterson, Frado appears as a "figure of resistance" who is "constructed by the Bellmonts as sexual and economic object."

The Wild Child's evolution from girl to woman is apparent in the twentieth-century African American narrative. However, the re-configuration of the Wild Child into the Wild Woman comes with various modifications: Although the Wild Woman remains motherless, she is no longer helpless. Though she is still sexualized, she resists being commodified. And although still mistreated, she can now fight back. The Wild Woman is no longer a caricature but rather a woman with character. She redefines notions of race and class and pushes beyond gender boundaries. She is secure, uninhibited, and articulate; most important, she is armed.

Whether literally or figuratively, the Wild Woman's weapons enable her to create and in some cases, re-create herself. The armor seems a form of empowerment through which the Wild Woman achieves both freedom and agency. The weapon of choice affords the Wild Woman the ability to connect or disconnect from the community at will as well as to fight back and regain her sense of identity. It is in this struggle for agency and power that the Wild Woman must improvise, and in so doing she learns that she has not only the ability to create but also the strength to break the barriers of silence and articulate herself.

The weapon of choice for the classic blues singer was the microphone. As Baraka's Clay notes, Bessie Smith used the microphone as a weapon against her oppressors by voicing her dissent in the coded language of her music: "They say, 'I Love Bessie Smith.' And don't even understand that Bessie Smith is saying, 'Kiss my ass, kiss my black unruly ass.' Before love, suffering, desire, anything you can explain, she's saying, and very plainly, 'kiss my black ass.' And if you don't know that it's you that's doing the kissing" (*Dutchman* 35). The microphone enabled Smith and other singers to express her desires as well as articulate her disapproval for the way Black women were being treated. Unlike the women of the blues tradition, who protested society's ills through song, the Wild Women of the literary jazz tradition are not easily granted such access to the microphone; instead, they must improvise other forms of armor to survive multiple layers of oppression.

In Jean Toomer's *Cane*, Karintha is armed by her beauty, which she is "carrying," "perfect as the dusk when the sun goes down" (Toomer 1143). Karintha illustrates the beginning of the transformation of the Wild Child into the Wild Woman. At the age of twelve, Karintha is "a wild flash that told the other folks just what it was to live" (Toomer 1143). Although Karintha is sexualized, she is not used as a commodity. She can also be characterized as motherless. Scholar Jennifer D. Williams contends that Karintha "can be read as the severance of a tie to origins, a move that serves a paradigmatic function for the remainder of the text. This originary break assumes the form of a foiled reproduction" (Williams 91). Those origins are reinscribed into the jazz tradition through saxophonist Marion Brown's 1973 trilogy of albums based on *Cane*, which includes a track titled "Karintha."[3] On "Karintha," Brown's solo drones while Bill Hasson reads from *Cane* in the background. Scholar Eric Porter notes that Brown "complicated the relationship between music and the written and spoken word" (Porter 252).

Similarly, Ann Petry's *The Street* includes a complex connection between music and language. Jazz vocalist Lutie Johnson remains both sexualized and objectified throughout the novel until she fights back, literally murdering her victimizer while symbolically killing a complex system of oppressive factors that undermines her power, destroys her sense of identity, and deprives her of agency. Although the novel refers to Granny, the ancestor figure, Lutie is motherless: Her mother was killed by "streets like 116th Street or being colored, or a combination of both with all it implied" (Petry 56). Living on 116th Street does not even afford Lutie a community of women. Lutie complains to herself that "there ought to be someone she could talk to, someone she could ask for advice," but her only consolation is the memory of Granny, who serves as a substitute mother (76). Although Lutie is without help, she is certainly not hopeless. She resolves to "fight back and never stop fighting back" (57). Yet her fighting back leads her to repeat the motherless tradition out of which she is born. Her murder of Boots leaves her child, Bub, motherless and alone.

Lutie can be read as a Wild Woman not only because of her out-of-control murderous act but also because women view her as a sexual deviant and men see her as an object of desire. Mrs. Chandler's women friends give her "queer, speculative look[s]" and express anxiety regarding her wild, unpredictable, sexually promiscuous behavior and their men: "Sure, she's a wonderful cook. But I wouldn't have any good-looking colored wench in my house. Not with John. You know they're always making passes at men. Especially white men. . . . Now I wonder—" (40–41). Although the word *wild* never appears, the allusion to wild promiscuity is clear. As scholar William Scott argues:

> Reading these passages merely as descriptions of stereotypi-cal thinking is not sufficient to account for the discourse of sexuality that motivates them. What they imply is that Lutie's

sexuality is defined as not only predictable but predictably unpredictable—uncontrollable, wild, or uncontainable—when she is in the presence of white men. Hence Petry's inclusion of a language of calculation or speculative guesswork to accompany the Chandlers' wondering: "queer, speculative look[s]," "that now-I-wonder look," "to verify their estimate[s]." The prostitute appears, then, as the appropriately combinatory figure to signify sex as calculation and economic calculation as sex. (Scott 98)

The figure of Lutie as sexual object is reinforced when Mrs. Hedges offers her a position as a prostitute and Boots proposes that Lutie sleep with Junto to obtain the money to extricate Bub from juvenile detention. According to Lutie, the association of Black women with licentiousness or prostitution was automatic:

> Queer how that was always cropping up. Here she was highly respectable, married, mother of a small boy, and, in spite of all that, knowing all that, these people took one look at her and immediately got that now-I-wonder look. Apparently it was an automatic reaction of white people—if a girl was colored and fairly young, why, it stood to reason she had to be a prostitute. If not that—at least sleeping with her would be just a simple matter, for all one had to do was make the request. In fact, white men wouldn't even have to do the asking because the girl would ask them on sight. (Petry 45)

In accordance with the gaze of Mrs. Chandler's community of white women, Mrs. Hedges, Boots Smith, Junto, and the Super, Lutie is viewed as having the potential to be a prostitute (sexually deviant) and thereby can be read as a Wild Woman. According to scholar Partha Miller, "Prostitutes and African women were placed in the same category, both as outsiders and as deviant, an embodiment of wild sexuality that was both feared and desired" (Miller 47).[4] Nevertheless, Lutie never allows herself to be commodified or used for profit. Instead, the mere association with prostitution and the physical mistreatment that she receives from Boots sets off a series of spontaneous actions that unveil her other wild side, which is characterized as an impulse to violence.

The novel opens with an air of violence as a prelude to the dramatic murder. The "cold November wind" is the aggressor, attacking both animate and inanimate objects on the street: "it rattled the tops of garbage cans, sucked window shades out through the top of opened windows and set them flapping back against the windows; and it drove most of the people off the street in the block between Seventh and Eighth Avenues except for a few hurried pedestrians who bent double in an effort to offer the least possible exposed surface to its violent assault" (Petry 1).

This violent assault echoes the end of the novel through Lutie's spontaneous, improvised murder of Boots Smith, an act committed by using the "candlestick as though it were a club" (430). The club refers to a billy club, a nonlethal weapon favored by cops, and is used as an instrument to police Boots. The club might also serve as a signifier for bebop: Just a year before the publication of *The Street*, Langston Hughes's fictional Jessie B. Semple remarks of the term *bebop* as originating from the sound of a billy club—the sound "beaten right out of some Negro's head into them horns and saxophones and piano keys that plays it." Thus, bebop sounds rooted in violence, and the music that emanates from the horns can be read as a form of resistance. Likewise, Lutie's violent murder of Boots constitutes resistance to the overwhelming reality of her position as helpless, sexualized object. Lutie's impulse to violence is motivated by her state of mind.

The murder seems framed within a psychological moment of insanity. Lutie becomes a Wild Woman who loses her sense of reality and is reduced to committing an act of barbarism for "even after he lay motionless, she kept striking him, not thinking about him, not even seeing him" (430). Lutie regains a sense of power through the act of killing Boots because she is striking out not only at him but also at the multiple oppressive layers he represents:

> First she was venting her rage against the dirty, crowded street . . .
> then the limp figure on the sofa became, in turn, Jim and the
> slender girl she'd found him with; became the insult in the

moist-eyed glances of white men on the subway; became the unconcealed hostility in the eyes of white women; became the greasy, lecherous man at the Crosse School for singers; became the gaunt Super pulling her down, down into the basement. Finally, and the blows were heavier, faster, now, she was striking at the white world which thrust black people into a walled enclosure from which there was no escape; and at the turn of events which had forced her to leave Bub alone while she was working so that he now faced reform school, now had a police record. (430)

Boots's murder enables Lutie to stitch a tapestry of victimizers that she battles (if only in her mind) and defeats: "She saw the face and head of the man on the sofa through waves of anger in which he represented all these things and she was destroying them" (430). Like improvisation, the spontaneous impulse to violence seems rooted in history and memory. The narrator makes clear that the violence is not only a sporadic episode of anger but is engendered by a history of subjugation and oppression that eventually implodes: "This impulse to violence had been in her for a long time, growing, feeding until finally she had blown up in a thousand pieces" (434).

Albert Murray regards this impulse to violence as the opposite of the blues. The type of murder that exceeds the limits of death, such as Bea Ella's knifing of Beau Beau Weavil and Lutie's bludgeoning of Boots, becomes no longer about the blues. Bea Ella's renaming as Red Ella makes a statement about her "biggest mistake of all," which is misunderstanding the true nature of the blues, and moves beyond the blues into the realm of the jazz aesthetic:

But Little Buddy and I knew that Papa Gumbo Willie Worthy had said red because what he was really talking about was the blues. Because he was responding to what Vanderbilt Coleman had said was Bea Ella Thornhill's biggest mistake of all: Not knowing that bad luck and disappointment meant not the end of the world but only that being human you had to suffer like everybody else from time to time. (122)

Bea Ella understood more about disappointment than anyone else and sought to somehow make the pain go away—and it did, for a moment. In that moment, like Lutie when she murders Boots, Bea Ella achieves power and a sense of agency. If, according to Ellison, the blues is "an impulse to keep the painful details alive in one's aching consciousness" (*Living with Music* 103), then jazz becomes the impulse to violence and a rejection of the painful details. The jazz impulse to violence involves a quest to (temporarily) remedy the blues. *Jazz* both articulates and complicates this impulse to violence.

Morrison's novel disrupts the narrative of the classic blues tradition by inserting the jazz figure of the armed Wild Woman during the 1920s. The narrator asserts that in 1926, "all over the country black women were armed" (*Jazz* 74); even women who were "unarmed" (77) still possessed their beliefs and ideology. However, "any other kind of unarmed black woman in 1926 was either silent or crazy or dead" (78). The novel's inscription of the armed Wild Woman into the 1920s, a period better known for its blues than for the renaissance of jazz in New York, suggests the overlap between the armed Wild Woman and the blues and jazz surrounding her.

It is significant that Morrison chooses to highlight 1926, a noteworthy year for African Americans and jazz music: John Coltrane was born, six-year-old Thelonious Monk became interested in piano, and Duke Ellington began to play "bona fide" jazz music in New York. Writing herself into this period, the narrator characterizes herself as "topnotch and indestructible—like the City in 1926 when all the wars are over and there will never be another one" (7). The city is inscribed into a modernist narrative, and the narrator Jazz becomes central to the Harlem Renaissance and the blues tradition. Yet this year is destructive as well. As the narrator notes:

Word was that underneath the good times and the easy money something evil ran the streets and nothing was safe—not even the dead. Proof of this being Violet's outright attack on the very subject of a funeral ceremony. Barely three days into 1926. A host of thoughtful people looked at the signs (the weather, the number, their own dreams) and believed it was the commencement of all sorts of destruction. Indeed something was lurking underneath and it shook the nation as the great depression unsettled the city and jolted American society into a harsh reality. (88)

Yet like Violet and Joe's relationship, what was lost in the late 1920s was recuperated later in the century. Similar to the blues transitioning into jazz, the licentious Wild Woman transformed into the armed Wild Woman.

Jazz begins with a telling inarticulacy: "Sth, I know that woman" (1). From the very beginning Morrison conjoins sound and sentiment signifying on the telling inarticulacy that characterizes the music and depicts the female voice as the progenitor of its sound.[5] Both the narrator and the sound that connects readers to the narrative are gendered female. Morrison portrays how womanhood is connected not only to the music but also to a wildness that is primitive (as in the characterization of Wild), at times licentious (Dorcas), and always armed (Violet). The novel links femininity to the violence inherent in the music: "A city seeping music that begged and challenged each and every day. Come, it said. Come and do wrong" (67). That Alice Manfred, Dorcas's aunt, is "no match" for the violent "race music" is no surprise because the narrator makes clear that the music not only serves as catalyst to violence, but promotes and urges violent action.

The presence of jazz connects to freedom and demands that one assume an aggressively defensive criminal posture—an aggressive criminality. The music "made you do unwise disorderly things. Just hearing it was like violating the law" (*Jazz* 58). As the music urges on violence, it is used as protection for men and a catalyst for women, and all can gain a sense of healing from listening, as evidenced at the end of the text, when Felice says that the "the music floated in to [Violet and Joe] through the open window" (214), and they began to dance together and asked Felice to join. Although she wanted to, she declined because something about their dancing made her feel that she "shouldn't be there. Shouldn't be looking at them doing that" (214). The dancing reinscribes the intimacy as well as repeats the motif of transition from the beginning of the novel, when they migrate from South to North and are described as "entering the lip of the city dancing all the way" (32). *Jazz* thus hints subtly at the music's sense of hopefulness without denying the inherent violence.

In the novel, jazz music is depicted not only as the impetus to violent acts but as violent and hostile in and of itself. Jazz can be read as a metaphor for the impulse to violence. Narrator Alice Manfred describes the music as having a "complicated anger . . . something hostile that disguised itself as flourish and roaring seduction" (59). Throughout the novel, seduction and anger intertwine as jazz is characterized as passionately violent, harmful, and disorderly. The "dirty get-on-down music" is the reason behind the "silent march," the murder of Dorcas, and Violet's slashing of the dead girl's face (6). Improvisation and violence characterize all of *Jazz's* Wild Women: Wild, Dorcas, Alice, Violet, and Felice. Together, these women can be read as representing the evolution of the African American Wild Woman from the nineteenth-century notion of Black women as wild spectacles to the twentieth-century reconstruction of the Wild Woman as artist/improviser.

Found in the woods by Golden Grey, Wild is the archetypal Wild Woman in nature. Wild is named by Hunters Hunter after she bites him when he attempts to cover her with a blanket. Unlike the Wild Women in mythology, Wild is not a witch; she is a "creature" without "the intelligence to be a witch," "powerless, invisible, and wastefully daft. Everywhere and nowhere" (179). Wild's omnipresence enables her to haunt the novel as a representation of motherlessness: "When for months there was no sign or sound of her, [Hunters Hunter] sighed and relived that time when his house was full of motherlessness— and the chief unmothering was Wild's" (167). Although Wild never speaks, she is often heard: she "groans" and "screams" from the cot before she gives birth (169). Hunters Hunter remembers her laugh "and how peaceful she was the first few days following the bite, so the touch of her fingertips didn't frighten him, but it did make him sad" (166).

Wild not only demonstrates the violent impulse, as evidenced in her bite, but also connects to the violent music of jazz through her telling inarticulacies, such as her laugh and her scream; Wild's way of communicating connects to nature's music. Joe describes Wild's music as the music of the world:

Once, after pulling ten trout in the first hours of dawn, Joe had walked past that place and heard what he first believed was some combination of running water and wind in high trees. The music the world makes, familiar to fishermen and shepherds, woodsmen have also heard. It hypnotizes mammals. Bucks raise their heads and gophers freeze. Attentive woodsmen smile and close their eyes. Joe thought that was it, and simply listened with pleasure until a word or two seemed to glide into the sound. Knowing the music the world makes has no words, he stood rock still and scanned his surroundings. . . . The scrap of song came from a woman's throat, and Joe thrashed and beat his way up the incline and through the hedge, a tangle of muscadine vines, Virginia creeper and hibiscus rusty with age. (176–77)

The "word or two" is her voice. All of the female figures in *Jazz* can be read as descendants of Wild. Wild Trace(s), or traces of Wild, appear in all the women, beginning with the trait of motherlessness.

Like the other Wild Women in the narrative, Violet's motherlessness bears a significant impact on how she relates to her partner. When she and Joe meet under the tree at night, he becomes the replacement mothering figure for her. Violet believes that "because their first conversation began in the dark (when neither could see much more of the other than silhouette) and ended in a green-and-white-dawn, nighttime was never the same for her. Never again would she wake struggling against the pull of a narrow well. Or watch first light with the sadness left over from finding Rose Dear in the morning twisted into water much too small" (104).

Violet's violent behavior and her subsequent forgiveness of Joe's action can be attributed to the fact that she is motherless—and worse, the child of a suicide. Like Lutie, Violet lacks a community of women, yet she searches for direction when she comes to the crossroads in her relationship with Joe. She says to Alice, "I'm fifty and I don't know nothing. What about it? Do I stay with him? I want to, I think. I want . . . well, I didn't always . . . now I want. I want some fat in this life. . . . Oh shoot! Where the grown people? Is it us?" (110). Alice responds by blurting out "Oh Mama," and then covering her mouth. This slip of the tongue seems a signifier for the motherlessness that all these women experience. Without mothers, there is a lack of community and of interpersonal relationships, since women have no one to turn to. Thus, in Joe's absence, Alice becomes Violet's surrogate mother.

Yet although these women can be seen as having traces of Wild, they inherit the music, which indoctrinates their impulse to violent and bizarre acts. Alice hears the "complicated anger in it, something hostile that distinguished itself as flourish and roaring seduction" (59). The rhythm and blues of the music seems a disguise, floating above an angry tempo that promises to boil over. Alice describes the music in terms of its "appetite" for violence:

> But the part she hated most was its appetite. Its longing for the bash, the slit; a kind of careless hunger for a fight or a red ruby stickpin for a tie—either would do. It faked happiness, faked welcome, but it did not make her feel generous, this juke joint, barrel hooch, tonk house, music. It made her hold her hand in the pocket of her apron to keep from smashing it through the glass pane to snatch the world in her fist and squeeze the life out of it for doing what it did and did and did to her and everybody else she knew or knew about. (59)

An implicit connection seems to exist between the hostile music and the historicized hostility of the African American woman. Yet it is not clear whether the music engenders the violence or the violence engenders the music. Like Ralph Ellison's *Invisible Man*, Alice believes that the music demand[s] action. However, as she points out to Violet, although the impulse to violence is present, taking action is a choice. Alice recalls her struggle to contain the impulse to violence after finding out that her husband had left her for another woman:

> Every day and every night for seven months she, Alice Manfred, was starving for blood. Not his. Oh, no. . . . Her craving settled on the red liquid coursing through the other woman's veins. . . . And maybe after galloping through seven months of nights on a horse she neither owned nor knew how to ride, over the twitching, pulpy body of a woman who wore white shoes

in winter, laughed loud as a child, and who had never seen
a marriage license—maybe she would have done something
wild. (86)

Although the impulse to violence is innate to humans, acting on
this impulse separates the Wild Woman from the ordinary woman.
Thus Alice questions Violet's audacious act of picking up a knife in
an attempt to distinguish herself and to remark on the choices that
women have. She tells Violet, "I don't understand women like you,
women with knives." When Violet replies, "I wasn't born with a knife,"
Alice retorts, "No, but you picked one up" (85). This dialogue gestures
toward the long-standing debate about whether violence is innate or
learned behavior. Here the women seem to agree that although the
impulse might be innate, the act is certainly a choice. For Alice, the art
of restraint needs finesse, because the impulse is everywhere; it can
be seen throughout the text as synonymous with music, as simple as
a phrase that might tiptoe out of a window: "Hit me but don't quit
me." As the narrator says,

> I have seen her, passing a café or an uncurtained window when
> some phrase or other—"Hit me but don't quit me"—drifted out,
> and watched her reach with one hand for the safe gathering rope
> thrown to her eight years ago on Fifth Avenue, and ball the other
> one into a fist in her coat pocket. I don't know how she did
> it—balance herself with two different hand gestures. But she
> was not alone in trying, and she was not alone in losing. It was
> impossible to keep the Fifth Avenue drums separate from the
> belt-buckle tunes vibrating from pianos and spinning on every
> Victrola. Impossible. (59)

As is the case for Wild, the music remains part of Alice and Violet's
environment and is inseparable from the innate impulse to violence.
Even without knowing the origins of the sound, the music spontaneously demands their attention and moves them to action. Unlike
Violet, Alice can contain the violent impulse that overtakes her
every time she hears the music. The music moves Joe in the right direction when he is seeking the wild girl Dorcas. After he finds her, he

spontaneously murders her as a consequence of the music he hears in the background. Likewise, the narrator believes that Violet's attempt to slash Dorcas's face also results from the music urging Violet on (79).

Violet's act of improvisation seems an out-of-body experience. Like Lutie, Violet experiences a moment of temporary disillusionment. Violet's alternate reality represents the degree to which improvisation can be viewed as a spontaneous occurrence akin to spirituality. Only able to recall what "that" Violet did, Violet tells her story in the third person. The creation of an alternate personality to describe a situation looks like a sign of trauma, similar to Pecola's downward spiral at the end of Morrison's *The Bluest Eye*. Unlike Pecola, however, Violet can fight back. The trauma of betrayal by her husband causes Violet to act on her impulse to violence by attempting to slash Dorcas's face. The slashing, which Alice calls an "insult," represents Violet's attempt to mark the young woman as a Wild Woman. Although Alice does not get a chance literally to mark Dorcas' face, Violet leaves her mark at the funeral, as Alice makes clear that all everyone talked about when they spoke of Dorcas was Viole(n)t. Thus the association of the Wild Woman with violence not only is implied through the image of Dorcas but is explicit in the community's renaming of the armed Wild Woman *Violent*.

The Wild Woman's impulse to violence in jazz fiction appears like improvisation in jazz music. The tension between the individual/improviser and the group becomes volatile as one instrument battles the other and each solo flight cries out for a response. In a sense, the interplay between the improviser/soloist and the group can be viewed as violent. In an effort to conjoin aspects of jazz music with their writings, writers of jazz fiction reconfigure the tension explicitly played out in the music throughout the narrative. The individual as improviser plays in the role of protagonist; the group dynamic is relegated to the insular community that populates the work of fiction; and the protagonist, in search of power and identity, must often use physical force to regain agency. This physical force is precipitated by the music—the impulse to violence.

In an interview with radio host Terry Gross, Morrison explains: "Part of the reason I was interested in [*Jazz*] and in this period was to figure out the impulse for violence as a notion of solution, and how it plays into notions of license and freedom." Both the impulse to violence and improvisation become spontaneous acts that rely on past experience and memory as a foundation for the action. Like the audience of the jazz jam session, the community/reader serves as judge and jury to the impulsive violent acts that occur in the text. For example, Petry and Morrison do not include government authority or any outsider into the insular community after the crimes are committed. Lutie flees, and Dorcas never names her assailant. Even Alice, who knows that Joe has murdered her niece, does not tell the police. The impulse to violence is not punished via the judicial system; rather, the community/reader/audience executes judgment.

According to a 1967 *Time* magazine article on "Violence in America," "The human impulse to violence cannot be completely denied or suppressed. When that is tried, the result is often an inner violence in man that can burst out all the more fiercely later." Both Lutie and Violet attempt to suppress the human impulse and thus exhibit inner turmoil (Lutie with her fantasy of the Super and Violet with the creation of an alter ego, "that Violet"). Yet both women ultimately make the choice when they go beyond the actual killing: Lutie by bludgeoning Boots long after he has stopped breathing and Violet by attempting to slash Dorcas's face at the funeral. The fact that these women continue the violent barrage after the victim is dead speaks to their motives. If they intended only to kill, they would have stopped as soon as the goal was achieved; in these cases, however, the act of killing becomes a symbolic assault that transcends the body of the actual victim and enters the realm of excess. Both authors seem to comment on the excessive nature of murder and violence. The impulse to violence for the Wild Woman indeed becomes a solution, albeit temporary, that gives her license and access to freedom.

Historically, the Wild Woman appears under various guises but is most notable as a sexual object. Whether in the form of seductress Lolita or licentious diva, the Wild Woman remains secure in her sexuality and makes it well known. Yet in African American women's literature, the image of the Wild Woman is constantly being reclaimed and appropriated, and she becomes both activist and improviser as she resists common patriarchal notions and creates a space for a new Black female-centered identity. This identity has always remained at the crossroads of normative definitions of womanhood. Black women have had to contend with the issues of multiple identities, ethnicities, and gender equality.

Tracing the historical representation of the Black female from wild object to improvising subject, we see the transformation of Black female identity through language and image as women authors reclaim the term Wild Woman and create a feminist discourse of power and resistance that moves beyond gender and sexuality. In the absence of sex and sexuality, Black women have a clear and present need to arm themselves and embody the connections among wildness, femininity, and jazz.

The women in these novels reconfigure from victims of circumstance to soloists with agency who obtain power through improvisation, which serves as a tool to refashion Black female identity. As improvisers, they push the boundaries set forth by the feminist agenda of the classic blues tradition and defy the normative/stereotypical perceptions of Black women as inarticulate and powerless as well as sexualized and subordinate.

Yet the moment of improvisation also complicates notions of Black female subjectivity by presenting the moment of power as temporary. Although the jazz moment of improvised violence creates a space for resistance and agency, its implicit brevity raises more questions than answers about the viability and reality of the Black female subject as truly independent and free. Like the elusiveness of the Wild Woman throughout literature, the jazz moment of improvisation is constantly being revised. Yet within the temporal moment of improvisation, what we read as an excessive act of capriciousness inscribes the Wild Woman as a powerfully dangerous armed subject. In constructed spaces where improvisation meets violence and gender garners power, Wild Women's voices echo through the loud, telling inarticulacies of improvised weapons of destruction.

Viewing the narrator as jazz personified, we can hear how the novel makes music as it interweaves the underlying rhythm of Wild Women on top of a melody that is complicated with intimate violence. At the end of the novel, Morrison asserts jazz's malleability and possibilities through the voice of the narrator. Thus, *jazz*'s cry at the end of the novel resounds as a call to action, encouraging readers not only to enter the discourse but to transform it—as the narrator states: "make me, remake me" (229).

Morrison situates this cry not only through a feminine voice but also with a feminist agenda. *Jazz* encourages women to freely participate in appropriating the music—"you are free to do it and I am free to let you" (229)—because the power of the music is now in the hands of her predominantly female readership: "look where your hands are. Now" (229).

Chapter 5

JAZZ AND THE CARIBBEAN

The Feminist Jazz Lens in Edwidge Danticat's
Breath, Eyes, Memory

Heralded Haitian American author Edwidge Danticat writes between
the lines of American and Caribbean culture by presenting characters
who travel between Haiti and the United States. Her first novel, *Breath,
Eyes, Memory* (1994), presents a family of women attempting to
discover their sexuality by challenging Haitian patriarchal traditions
and ultimately reclaiming their bodies within an American ideological framework. Danticat infuses the novel with a jazz ethos that
enables countless variations portraying the loss of sexuality through
rape and abuse, the denial of sexuality through a communal silence,
and the reclamation of sexuality through a spiritual purging of
memory.

The protagonist Sophie Caco travels back and forth from Haiti to
New York in an effort to understand the legacy of the sexual abuse
endured by generations of her family's women. Sophie's quest becomes
a matter of gaining control over her body and finding her own identity
by adapting to American culture. Danticat adopts jazz as a marker for
American culture and freedom by using the music as a catalyst for
acts of transgression. In the end, Sophie attains freedom through the
music by affirming a new hybrid cultural identity that draws on both
Old and New World traditions. Reading the Caribbean narrative
through a jazz lens enables us to see how the cultural appropriation
of such elements as oral traditions, the archetype of the Wild Woman,
and intimate violence into the Caribbean context aid in the (re)con-
struction of an intercultural female identity and ultimately present a
new hybrid genre, the Caribbean American jazz novel.

The attempt to place a jazz lens onto a Caribbean novel may seem counterintuitive. Jazz music is primarily recognized as an American art form created by African Americans. Known to many as America's classical music, jazz possesses democratic ideals and roots within the period of slavery that make it quintessentially African American and part of the American protest music tradition.[1] So what does jazz music have to do with Caribbean culture and literature? If jazz is indeed a descendant of the blues, then its diasporic lineage can be traced through slavery to find an African aesthetic within its musical rituals. What became known as jazz music by the early twentieth century enabled the emotional and spiritual freedom necessary for a dislocated and dispossessed population of African slaves to adapt and sustain themselves. Thus, it is no surprise that, at the most fundamental level of communication via call-and-response, traces of the music can be found in the literature of the African diaspora. Explaining how jazz can be viewed as geographically boundless by means of its global influence throughout the diaspora, scholar Travis Jackson notes, "Jazz was not born in a vacuum. . . . [W]hat we call jazz was created in that movement of people and commodities through the Caribbean, Western Europe, and the United States. It is the music of the African Diaspora" (qtd. in Carnig).

Breath, Eyes, Memory highlights the connection between jazz music and the Caribbean and more specifically the distinct relationship between jazz music and Haitian culture. Indeed, jazz, a music of emancipation and freedom, holds definite connections to the world's first free Black republic. After Haitian independence in 1804, many people left the island and settled in New Orleans, the birthplace of jazz, and as Zora Neale Hurston has pointed out, jazz contains traces of Haitian religious culture, specifically voodoo.

Through the incorporation of various elements of Haitian voodoo and the presence of jazz, Danticat's novel creates a complex inter-connection among orality, jazz music, and Haitian religious traditions. Hence, the jazz lens becomes the most appropriate critical tool for uncovering the ways in which Danticat attempts to subvert various Haitian cultural traditions and thereby aid women in achieving autonomy through acts of resistance, revision, and reconstruction.

This chapter takes interest in the transculturated artifact of jazz and the ideologies inspired by the music that Sophie adopts in America through her husband Joseph.[2] Joseph, a major proponent of the jazz ethos, becomes the catalyst that initiates Sophie's sexual awakening and her subsequent freedom. This chapter underscores a jazz ethos that is based on a jazz aesthetic. To this end, the insertion of jazz as symbol into the Caribbean American narrative includes not only the music but also a jazz tradition rooted in an American cultural environment that informed the lives of community members. By *ethos* I mean the fundamental character or spirit of a culture, the underlying sentiment that undergirds the beliefs, customs, or practices of a group—in this case, the African diaspora. The jazz ethos is characterized by the American ideals of freedom, democracy, and improvisation. These ideals are championed by Joseph and by the Haitian voodoo goddess of love Erzulie.[3]

Joseph, an African American jazz musician, represents the bridge between the dislocated diasporic identities. Throughout the novel, jazz serves as both a symbolic and literal vehicle to undergird the idea of a united diaspora in the United States, despite the reality of the tension that may exist between ethnic identities. According to scholar Robert Fox, "the Diaspora is a series—indeed a tangle—of crossroads. The crossroads is a tricky, and even dangerous, place, but it has the advantage of being a site from which one can look in many directions at once. . . . Meaning is both made and unmasked here (in short there is a signifying on all levels), and it is here that hybridity happens" (370).

Hybridity occurs not only within a cultural context but within a musical matrix. In the novel, jazz emerges as a hybrid music with various cultural influences that is constantly being revised. Jazz represents the idea of what Fox describes as diasporacentrism, "the articulation of a 'centerless center' aimed at troubling the inward whirl of centrisms that tend to be unnatural focuses, retroactive and overdetermined. Diasporacentrism, on the other hand is mobile, fluid, indeterminate" (368). As represented through Joseph, jazz becomes decentered and, despite its roots, remains always en route as it transforms and continuously unfolds into new sounds of meaning and representation. Both jazz's symbolic and literal roots are reconstructed. Fox elaborates that jazz's origins are rooted in a hybrid culture: "Whatever other constructions have since come into play regarding its identity, jazz in its origins, is Creole" (372).

Like jazz, Joseph was born in New Orleans, and he identifies himself as a Creole. As scholar Yolanda Pierce notes, Joseph "is not only African American, he is Creole. . . . Creoles are ethnically a mix of French, Spanish, African and Native American, similar to the ethnic variety of Haitian people" (Pierce 77). Like New Orleans and jazz music, Joseph is a product of diasporic influences.

A musician, Joseph likes to play "slave songs, Negro spirituals, both on his saxophone and his piano, slowing them down or speeding them up at different tempos" (Danticat 71). He idolizes Charlie Parker and Miles Davis and frequently plays at the "Note," a shortening of the name of Manhattan's famous jazz club the Blue Note. Joseph can be seen as a jazz symbol due to the various signifiers that associate him with the music and as a jazzman because of his easy improvisational lifestyle. He tells Sophie, "It's okay not to have your future on the map, that way you can flow wherever life takes you." Sophie's response signals the great cultural divide between them: she labels Joseph a "wanderer" and describes his lifestyle as "very American." And Joseph replies, "I am African-American. The African. It means that you and I, we are already part of each other" (72). Joseph's understanding of the interrelations between peoples of the African diaspora informs his response to Sophie and his musical quest for the diasporic connection he hears in jazz.

Joseph travels throughout the diaspora attempting to understand the interrelationships among African American music and music from the islands. He has traveled to "Jamaica, Cuba, and Brazil several times trying to find links between the Negro Spirituals and Latin and island music" (73). Joseph takes interest in various kinds of music. He buys albums from the Haitian music store and listens to the "drum and conch shell beats" with Sophie. Historically, the conch shell and the drums served as forms of communication— specifically for call-and-response among slaves.[4] Joseph, like the music, bridges the various diasporic identities. His marriage to So- phie both complicates and resolves the tension in West Indian and African American relations, putting him at odds with Sophie's mother

Martine. By the end of the novel, however, Martine realizes that they are connected spiritually through the music.

Over dinner, Martine and Joseph establish a connection through the music. After Joseph tells Martine that he is from Louisiana and knows Creole, she says, "I feel like I could have been Southern" (214). Martine clarifies that she is asserting a deeper connection than simply a common African ancestor; rather, she locates herself within the southern religious traditions of African Americans and ascribes that connection to religious songs: "Non, non, me in particular. I feel like I could have been Southern African-American. When I just came to this country, I got it into my head that I needed some religion. I used to go to this old Southern church in Harlem where all they sang was Negro spirituals" (215). Martine is signifying on the Great Migration, which parallels her own immigration: according to *The Encyclopedia of the Harlem Renaissance*, "at the close of the great migration in the late 1960's, Harlem had become a Southern and Caribbean city. Most of its people spoke with southern or Caribbean accents, they prepared and ate traditional southern and Caribbean foods, their worship services conformed to southern and Caribbean conventions" (Wintz and Finkelman 442).

Harlem is both a symbol and literal location for the congregants of the Black diaspora. Harlem becomes home to transplanted Africans from all parts of the diaspora, a safe space that houses southern religious traditions within the northern landscape and where a young Haitian woman feels connected to the music and what it ultimately represents—freedom and perseverance.

Over dinner, Martine asks Joseph to explain to Marc what exactly a Negro Spiritual is: "You tell him, Joseph. Tell this old Haitian, with his old ways, about a Negro spiritual." Joseph responds:

They're like prayers . . . hymns that slaves used to sing. Some were happy, some sad, but most had to do with freedom, going to another world. Sometimes that other world meant home, Africa. Other times it meant Heaven, like it says in the Bible. More often it meant freedom. Joseph began to hum a spiritual. Oh Mary, don't you weep! That's a Negro Spiritual, said my mother. It sounds like a Voudou song, said Marc. He just

described a Voudou song. Erzulie, don't you weep. He sang
playfully. I told you I could have been southern. My mother
laughed. (Danticat 215)

The passage emphasizes the interconnectedness between Haitian and
African American music, and although Marc is not familiar with
Negro spirituals per se, he recognizes its analogue in Haitian voodoo.
Thus the Negro spiritual and the voodoo song become one and the
same, distinguished only in name. Martine is thus correct: She could
indeed have been southern, because the southern religious experience
is also part of her ancestry.

The dinner ends with Martine's improvisational rendition of
"Motherless Child." As she rocks her granddaughter Brigitte, she
solemnly sings the spiritual. Martine recognizes that spirituals tell
not of the individual journey but rather of a collective experience.
Martine requests that dinner guests "help me if I stumble" (220).
Everyone seated at the table is in some respect a motherless child:
Marc is disconnected from his mother country, Haiti; both of Joseph's
parents died before he was fifteen (73); Sophie is twice abandoned
by her mother and must abandon her own child to return to Haiti
and confront the ghosts of her past; Martine both abandons her
mother Grandma Ife, and flees her motherland Haiti, after the rape.
Martine's singing expresses a cry that represents the community's
literal and symbolic distance and disconnection from home. Thus, all
the members of Martine's family feel a connection to the lyrics and
the song and affirm her cry with applause: As Sophie states, "We all
clapped when she was done, Brigitte too" (215).

As Sophie relates, "On the ride back to Providence, Joseph kept
singing my mother's spiritual, adding some bebop to the melody, as
though to reverse the sad tone" (216). Sophie's comment acknowledges
that although the song might resonate with her and the others, it is
ultimately her mother's spiritual. Joseph's revision and insertion of
new rhythms characterizes him as a child of the jazz tradition and a
champion of the jazz ethos. For Joseph, the spirituals present a myriad
of possibilities through repetition, improvisation, and reconstruction.
The repetition and the addition of various jazz melodies not only rec-
reate but also redefine the song, mitigating its overall solemnity and

infusing it with the jubilation of hope and freedom that the bebop era represented.

Joseph's music resounds throughout the narrative and it is the sound of his music that engenders Sophie's sexual awakening: "I heard him playing his keyboard as I lay awake in bed. The notes and scales were like raindrops, teardrops, torrents. I felt the music rise and surge, tightening every muscle in my body. Then I relaxed, letting it go, feeling a rush that I knew I wasn't supposed to feel" (76). The music rises and surges throughout Sophie's body and allows her to feel something forbidden. Sophie's newfound bodily pleasure leads to her daily visits with Joseph: "At first I would sit on the linoleum and listen to him play. Then slowly, I moved closer until sometimes he would let me touch the keyboard, guiding my fingers with his hand on top of mine. Between strokes, I learned the story of his life" (73). Danticat's description of Sophie and Joseph's sexual interaction places the music in relation to a forbidden sexuality. Martine learns that Sophie has been engaging with a man and begins the traditional testing to ensure that Sophie remains pure. These tests maintain the mother's control over the daughter's body and ensure that Sophie remains a virgin until she is given away in marriage.

During Sophie's first test, Martine uses storytelling to distract Sophie from the incestuous act she is about to perform. Martine's narrative involves the marassas (twins) who are "inseparable lovers" (84). For Martine, the marassas represent her relationship with Sophie, and Joseph's presence is demonized. He is an interloper who threatens to rob Sophie of her honor. The countless tests eventually lead to Sophie's jazz moment of improvisational violence.

While listening to Joseph's saxophone wailing into the night, Sophie decides to end the testing by using a pestle to destroy the "veil that always held my mother's finger back every time she tested me" (88). Sophie's jazz moment of improvisation occurs after she essentially ends her relationship with Joseph. Since the testing began, Sophie has been ignoring his phone calls, and she would rather deny their relationship than deal with the fact that it is the cause of the sexual abuse that she must endure weekly. Sexual violence and love are conflated, and the music, represented by Joseph, serves as the catalyst for that conflation. As in Cholly's jazz moment of improvisation, the conflation of violence, music, and love conjoins with domesticity and feelings of isolation. Yet unlike Cholly's moment, which occurs within the domestic space of the kitchen, Sophie, like Violet, Lutie, and other Wild Women, transforms a domestic object into a weapon:

> I twirled the ring around my finger listening to the saxophone wailing in the dark. My mother rarely spoke to me since she began the tests. When she went out with Marc I refused to go and she showed no desire to take me along. I was feeling alone and lost, like there was no longer any reason for me to live. I went down to the kitchen and searched my mother's cabinet for the mortar and pestle we used to crush spices. I took the pestle to bed with me and held it against my chest. (87)

Danticat's use of jazz coupled with the promise ring from Joseph in the beginning of this scene underscores the ideological influence of Joseph and his music on Sophie. The poster of Charlie Parker and Miles Davis on her wall gives credence to the wail of Joseph's music. The wail or cry is a lament of sorts, deriving from Joseph's saxophone. It is a mourning cry for Parker's sound and the resistance to the more traditional forms of jazz that characterized the bebop movement. The saxophone wail might sound like a mourning cry to the image of Davis, a figure who also looms over Sophie and suggests the paradoxical nature of the moment.

Critics have noted an alluring femininity in Davis's music as well as the violent abuse he inflicted on the women's bodies he caressed each night. In her eloquent critique of Miles Davis, "Ladies Sing Miles," scholar Farah Jasmine Griffin notes the contradictions between the man and his music: "In the sounds that emanate from Miles there is space for tears, vulnerability, anger, love, sexuality, creativity; a space simply to be." Yet his image on Sophie's wall, devoid of the sound of his music, also suggests a betrayal. As Griffin notes, because his music seemed to provide such "a safe place," many women "felt so betrayed by his admission of emotional, verbal, and physical violence against women."

Sophie's mother represents similar contradictions. The home provided by Martine, like Davis's music, is the safe space in which

Sophie finds both shelter and nourishment. But it is violated by what are supposed to be the nurturing hands of her mother. Martine's violation of that space causes Sophie to feel betrayed and alone. The safe space of the home, and to a larger extent the bedroom, becomes filled with the violence as well as the alluring feminine qualities of the music. The wail emanating from Joseph's saxophone signals a call to action. Danticat's use of jazz to preface Sophie's act of transgression suggests that, as *Jazz's* Alice Manfred put it, something about the music beckons a person to "come and do wrong" (Morrison *Jazz* 67).

Within the framework of music, this telling scene also speaks to the loneliness and isolation Sophie feels despite her geographical location in New York City. Sophie seems devoid of a community of women, and her only companions remain at a distance. She is separated from Joseph not only by physical distance but also by the psychological space imposed by the breakup; she is separated from her mother by the tension resulting from the testing. Her feelings of isolation lead her to believe that "there was no longer any reason for me to live" (Danticat 86). Here, Sophie's thoughts of suicide foreshadow her death and subsequent rebirth, as she parallels her story to that of the bleeding woman.

Before Sophie begins the process of self-abuse, she doubles by telling herself the story of a woman who goes to Erzulie for a transformation so that she will stop menstruating. This transformation would mean that the woman would no longer be a woman, so she must choose a different life form. The woman opts to be a butterfly, a symbol of freedom, and never bleeds again. Sophie, too, will also choose freedom over the cultural bondage of womanhood. The image of Sophie holding the pestle to her heart recalls Erzulie with a knife to her heart. Like the woman in the parable, Sophie's attempt to stop the pain of the testing will bear consequences that equate to the loss of womanhood yet will also lead to her freedom. Unlike the bleeding woman's blood, which signifies on female genitalia and ultimate womanhood by means of menstrual bleeding, Sophie's blood is meant to suggest a Christlike sacrifice:

My flesh ripped apart as I pressed the pestle into it. I could see the blood slowly dripping onto the bed sheet. I took the pestle and the bloody sheet and stuffed them into a bag. It was gone, the veil that always held my mother's finger back every time she *tested* me. My body was quivering when my mother walked into the room to test me. My legs were limp when she drew them aside. I ached so hard I could hardly move. Finally I failed the test. (88)

Sophie's symbolic death looks like a sacrifice that she makes to avoid continual suffering from the testing, and it informs her decision not to pass on such a traumatic tradition. Her choice of the pestle reminds us of the domestic ideology that characterizes womanhood in Haitian culture. Both Sophie and her aunt Tante Atie resist the patriarchal cultural traditions of domesticity. Sophie loses her womanhood as it is defined in Haitian cultural terms, using her hands to perform an act of resistance rather than the domestic duties required of women. The act of stuffing both pestle and bloody sheet into the bag signifies not only on her resistance toward the domestic traditions of her culture but also on the long-standing Haitian patriarchal tradition that men hang the blood-stained sheets of their virgin brides as a symbol of pride, conquest, and power. In this moment, discarding the traditions that reinforce the patriarchal order, Sophie does indeed kill a part of her "Haitian" self. Awaiting the judgment of her mother, Sophie's body shakes with the pain and fear of her bold defiance.

Sophie's act of transgression can be read as directed not only at her mother but also at the generations of women who allowed such violence to continue. When Sophie seeks answers from Grandma Ife about the continual testing and the lack of protest by generations of Caco women, she replies that tradition and community exude a force that is greater than the individual and that a mother's job is to keep her daughter pure:

If a child dies, you do not die, but if your child is disgraced, you are disgraced. And people, they think daughters will be raised trash with no man in the house. . . . From the time a girl begins to menstruate to the time you turn her over to her husband, the mother is responsible for her purity. If I give a soiled daughter to her husband, he can shame my family, speak evil of me, even bring her back to me. (156)

Thus, the act of testing is part of the patriarchal tradition that ensures that women remain virgins until marriage. This practice solely reflects the man's need for respect and denies women the right to their own bodies. A woman's body, protected by her mother when she is a child and given away to her husband when she reaches adulthood, appears to be compelling evidence of the lack of agency granted Haitian women. Thus, the practice of testing is brought over to the United States, and the same ideology informs how Martine deals with Sophie's relationship with Joseph.

Sophie's ideological and spiritual awakening via the jazz ethos propels her to challenge this tradition, and she not only resists it but reconstructs it. Her mutilation bears witness to a legacy of incestuous violence, yet revises the tradition within a New World landscape. In America, Sophie holds the option to possess authority over her own body and the possibility to break free from old traditions. After Sophie fails the test, Martine believes that she has failed to protect Sophie's purity and banishes her from the house. Sophie's decision to marry Joseph seems an attempt to mitigate the emotional pain she is feeling and to pursue "happiness" in a place called Providence, Rhode Island. Yet Sophie's literal and psychological wound from the pestle takes time to heal.

Although Joseph is a proponent of the jazz ethos, even he does not understand the potential repercussions of the transculturated ideals of freedom, democracy, and improvisation for a young Haitian woman in America. As Sophie remarks, "I had spent two days in the hospital with stitches between my legs. Joseph could never understand why I had done something so horrible to myself. I could not explain to him that it was like breaking manacles, an act of freedom" (130). Sophie remains traumatized emotionally by the memory of the abuse. Female sexual violence and abuse take on various forms in the novel. The testing parallels Martine's rape in the cane fields, as both she and Sophie suffer from nightmares that are attributed to their traumas.

The trope of incestuous rape recurs throughout twentieth-century African American literature, including within the Caribbean

American context. Danticat exposes mother-daughter incest as an established occurrence, and though particular to Sophie's experience, it is indicative of a culture that privileges the purity and sanctity of the female body over the physical and psychological wellness of a woman's spirit. Sophie describes it as a "virginity cult"—mothers' "obsession" with keeping their daughters "pure and chaste" (154). This practice produces generations of women who sexually abuse their daughters. Grandma Ife recognizes the history of abuse, apologizing for the pain she has caused Sophie and handing her a statue of Erzulie to serve as Sophie's guide and protector. Erzulie functions throughout the text as the protector of tormented spirits, emblem and signifier of the wild spirit of resistance that the women in the novel seek to emulate.

Erzulie is one of the most complex figures in Caribbean mythology. She wears various faces as the ideal of both the best and worst parts of womanhood. Anthropologist Claudine Michel notes, "Erzulie represents sexuality, lesbianism and motherhood" (Michel and Bellgarde-Smith 36).[5] She exhibits the type of freedom sought by all of the Caco women. The goddess appears in the novel via myths, symbols, and references, and her sexual proclivities, her primitive protective spirit, and her armed appearance mark her as a Wild Woman. In "Erzulie: A Women's History of Haiti," literary critic Joan Dayan explains: "She is called the loa of 'love' but she demands that we re-invent the word. As desire for what has been stunted by the minds of men, she forces us to enter a world where the word is undone, where certain tenants [*sic*] of affection or attachment undergo some strange, instructive, metamorphoses" (Dayan 10). These tenets of affection or attachment that undergo strange, instructive metamorphoses appear not only between Sophie and her mother but also between Louise and Tante Atie. They can be read as the cultural taboo of same-sex relationships. Although Erzulie is said to be patron saint of homosexuals, lesbian relationships remain frowned on within the Haitian cultural environment, to the extent that Grandma Ife moans, "The gods will punish me for [my daughter] Atie's ways" (Danticat 167).

Although the novel never names the tension between Grandma Ife and Atie, it is implied through Grandma Ife's dislike of Louise, a young "friend" who gives Atie reading lessons at night. The novel subtly shows the reader that Atie does much more than read with Louise. As scholar Myriam Chancy points out: Atie's "relationship with Louise is in fact subtly coded as a lesbian love relationship. Although there is the merest hint that the two are not sexually involved, suggested through numerous scenes in which Louise leaves at sundown and in which the two only come together at daylight, theirs is undoubtedly an erotic relationship" (37). Interestingly, Atie uses the coded word *friend* to describe her relationship with Louise, and the same term appears throughout the text to denote sexual relationships. Sophie's therapist, Rena, decodes the term when Sophie is describing her mother's relationship with her longtime lover Marc.

Danticat's critique of a heteronormative cultural environment emerges through the transgressive statements made by Tante Atie. When discussing womanhood, Atie makes clear that women are raised to obey the patriarchal laws of domesticity represented by their "ten fingers," yet she wishes that an additional two might be granted for her own purposes:

> According to Tante Atie, each finger had a purpose. It was the way she had been taught to prepare herself to become a woman. Mothering. Boiling. Loving. Baking. Nursing. Frying. Healing. Washing. Ironing. Scrubbing. It wasn't her fault, she said. Her ten fingers had been named for her even before she was born. Sometimes she even wished she had six fingers on each hand so she could have two left for herself. (Danticat 151)

In Haitian cultural traditions, women are raised to be conscious of their duty to men. As Sophie states, "The men in this area, they insist that their women are virgins and have ten fingers" (151). Thus, the female body is always already relegated to the domestic sphere. Atie's resistance to home life and her constant wandering through the night underscore her refusal to be contained by traditional norms (111). Further, Atie's reading lessons with Louise aid in the formation of a new coded language that Louise describes as poetry.

Atie's poems deploy coded language to describe her acts of transgression and enable her to express her desires privately within the pages of her notebook and through the indecipherable meaning of her words. Reading and writing enables Atie to find freedom. In

Sophie's words, "I think it is very good that she has learned how to read. . . . It is her own freedom" (119). Yet, as Grandma Ife points out, "Tante Atie has changed a lot. . . . [T]he reading, it is only one thing" (119). Atie's freedom comes not only from language but also from her sexuality, and the two go hand in hand. Atie's poems involve her deepest feelings—her maternal love for Sophie and her intimate love for Louise.

Atie's poems can be understood as the written form of *pale andaki* (a Haitian Creole form of code switching), and its appearance in parables and other literary devices in the novel highlights the tension between individuals and language. Danticat uses parables to subvert the violent nature of the actions that take place. *Pale andaki* turns into doubling as Sophie recounts stories to help her cope with the traumatic experience of being tested, and it underscores Grandma Ife's role as ancestor figure. In addition, Atie uses the principles of *pale andaki* to code the poem that describes her intimate relationship with Louise:

> She speaks in silent voices, my love.
> Like the cardinal bird, kissing its own image [. . .]
> I drink her blood with milk
> And when the pleasure peaks, my love leaves. (134–35)

The silent voice that her love speaks refers to the act of reading: only through reading can one hear voices in silence, and only through writing can one speak in silence. Louise's reading lessons both literally and figuratively introduce Atie to a new language. Literally, it is French, the language of the colonizer: "Louise had helped her paraphrase the poem from a book of French poetry that Louise had read when she was still in school" (135). Figuratively, it is a new language that allows her to speak herself into existence. Atie becomes the figure who speaks her own voice, as she becomes the "cardinal bird, kissing its own image." As Atie explains, "Our family name, Caco, it is the name of a scarlet bird. A bird so crimson, it makes the reddest hibiscus or the brightest flame trees seem white" (150). The reference to kissing its own image also recalls the Marassas, "two inseparable lovers" (84), as well as Atie's relationship with Louise, since the two are inseparable:

"We are like milk and coffee, lips and tongue. We are two fingers on the same hand. Two eyes on the same head" (98).

The third line, "Li pale vwa mwin" (he/she/it speaks my voice)—the only line that is not translated into English—can be read in various ways. The Creole term *li* can mean *he, she*, or *it* and thus refer back to the language that speaks her voice—in this case, the Creole language. Or it can refer to the way in which Louise speaks her voice. Again, the *andaki* dialect allows multiple meanings, and the true meaning can be deciphered only by the intended audience. Thus, speaking the same language as the poem is vital for communication: the images in the next three lines are not only sounds but language with double meaning. Flapping wings can refer to a Haitian proverb, "Parole Gin Pie Zel. The words can give wings to your feet," that Grandma Ife recalls at the end of the novel. Words giving wings to one's feet can communicate a change or perhaps indicate that freedom is the key to riches. Likewise, the broken bottles indicate fragmentation, while the whistling snakes evoke trepidation. Finally, the "boom bang" drums allude not only to music but also to a native sound of communication via call-and-response. This image recalls the sound Danticat incorporates elsewhere to indicate the various methods of communication: "Drums throbbing in the distance and some staccato conch shells answering the call" (136).

The poem's final three lines offer a repetition with a slight variation. Here "my love" seems to refer to Louise, signaling their sexual union through a reversal of the parable of the young husband who kills his young bride because he wants to prove her virginity to the community. According to Chancy, "The last two lines of the poem echo the traditional tale except that Atie has taken the place of the male hero; she occupies his position but is not male-identified" (Chancy 131). In addition, these lines present a new tale of sexual intimacy between two women. Not only does the I in the poem "drink her blood with milk," which subtly puns on the act of lesbianism as "the pleasure peaks," but the I is also left alone and abandoned. The poem foreshadows Louise's departure, her decision to live and be free.

Atie's intimate relationship with Louise contrasts with Atie's relationship with Monsieur Augustin, a handsome neighbor. However, both of these relationships are out of reach due to the traditional gender and class norms imposed on Haitian culture. Through the coded language of Atie's poetry as well as in other places in the novel, Danticat's narrative techniques reinforce the cultural silence that discourages intimate relationships outside of class and gender norms. Atie's poems, read aloud and inserted into the text for the reader's pleasure, like *pale andaki* resist such codes by eluding meaning and showing language's potential to communicate at multiple levels. Tante Atie's revision of the story of the man and his new wife is an attempt to reconstruct her own story in a way that acknowledges her relationship with Louise through poetic narrative, out loud, but paradoxically within a silenced voice.

Tante Atie is not the only female figure who mirrors aspects of Erzulie; Sophie's imagination casts her mother as Erzulie. Martine exhibits qualities and undertakes actions that support the theory that she is more like Erzulie than any other character. Dayan describes Erzulie as of mixed race, and to this end Martine purchases beauty products that lighten the complexion of her skin—so much so that the change is noticeable when she returns to Haiti. Her attempts to attribute the lightening to the weather in New York, where the cold makes her look like a ghost, are dismissed, and her mother asks whether Martine uses facial products. Martine is seeking to change her image, exhibiting a self-hatred that compares to Sophie's self-hatred, which results in her bulimia. Both complexes dealing with the body relate to the traumatic abuse experienced by women.

Iconic images of Erzulie show her as a protector, carrying a child in one hand and a knife in the other. Danticat creates a character that seems to resemble the figure but performs actions that are contrary to what Erzulie represents. Martine falls short of this image in two respects. First, too traumatized by the rape to remain in Haiti, she fails to protect her daughter Sophie. Second, when Martine becomes pregnant again (this time through consensual sex), she uses the knife to harm rather than protect the child. After Martine learns that she is pregnant, the nightmares of the rape become more vivid, and her hatred of her body increases. After she hears the baby speaking to her, she decides to obtain an abortion (Danticat 217). The red that makes up the color palette of her apartment foreshadows the blood that is spilled by her suicide.

Martine's final words, "*Mwen pa Kapab encore*" (I cannot go on anymore), demonstrate her refusal to go on in the face of her hardships. These hardships, which scholar Albert Murray would define as the blues, lead her to act of violence, and it turns not only inward, as she kills herself, but also outward toward what she believes is the source of her trauma, the rapist. As Martine contemplates an abortion, Sophie becomes worried because Martine has begun to hear voices, particularly that of the baby: "It has a man's voice, so now I know it's not a girl. . . . Everywhere I go, I hear it." She hears the baby speaking in the rapist's voice, "saying things to me. . . . He calls me filthy whore" (217).

These voices seem a sign of posttraumatic stress disorder, which affects both Martine and Sophie as a consequence of the sexual abuse they have endured. The novel reveals a generational as well as a cultural attitude toward therapy. Whereas Sophie works with a counselor to resolve her issues, Martine relies on God and the community; and after leaving for the United States, Martine's only source of community is Sophie. Martine feels comfortable telling her daughter about her nightmares as well as the voices, and Sophie seems to understand, telling her therapist that her mother has been living with the rape for years and that she has survived by faking her happiness: "That's always how she's survived. She feels that she has to stay one step ahead of a mental institution so she has to hold it together at least on the surface" (218). The therapist's proposal that Martine perform an exorcism rather than an abortion is never realized. Martine stabs herself the same day as she stabs the baby whom she believes to have the voice of her victimizer.

Sophie attempts to empower her mother on her death bed by dressing her in colors reminiscent of Erzulie:

> It was too loud a color for a burial. I knew it. She would look like a Jezebel, hot-blooded Erzulie who feared no men, but rather made them her slaves, raped them, and killed them. She was the only woman with that power. It was too bright a red for burial. If we had an open coffin at the funeral home, people would talk. It was too loud a color for burial but I chose it. (227)

Although Erzulie is being discussed, Sophie's language denotes a blues-like repetitive AAB form. The first line "It was too loud a color for burial" is repeated with a difference, "It was too bright a red for burial," and finally concludes with "It was too loud a color for burial but I chose it." The subtle infusion of the blues through Sophie's narration, as she discusses the interconnections between Erzulie and Martine, inscribes all three women into the jazz musical tradition. Martine thus becomes a wild woman "buried in clothes the color of flames" (234). Further, Martine's death is foreshadowed by Erzulie's tears.

Sophie visits the house of Davina, one of the women in her sex therapy group, to pray to Erzulie:

> I went in and sat in the dark and drank some verbena tea by candlelight. The flame's shadows swayed across Erzulie's face in a way that made it seem as though she was crying. On the way out, I saw Buki's balloon. It was in a tree, trapped between two high branches. It had deflated into a little ball the size of a green apple. We thought it had floated into the clouds, even hoped that it had traveled to Africa, but there it was slowly dying in a tree right above my head. (221)

Although many scholars conclude that Erzulie's weeping is incomprehensible,[6] here it foreshadows the paradoxical tears of death, at once sorrowful that the person has passed yet content that he or she is no longer suffering. Sophie's prayer to Erzulie parallels the balloon's release, hinting at a critique of the effects of exorcism and prayer for the traumatized victim—flung upward yet ultimately never reaching its intended destination.

Danticat's novel reveals two coping methods for trauma victims that transcend cultural and traditional Haitian norms: therapy and the sexual phobia group. Buki, an Ethiopian college student who was genitally mutilated by her grandmother at puberty, releases the balloon in honor of the three women, Buki, Sophie, and Davina, a middle-aged Chicana who was raped by her father for ten years. The sexual phobia group unites women of the diaspora under one cause: the impact of a traumatizing adolescent past on adult women. Buki's balloon represents freedom, a release of past traumas with the intention of embracing the future. As Sophie notes, "We went to Davina's backyard and watched as [Buki] released [the balloon] in the dark. It was hard to see where the balloon went but at least it had floated out of our hands. I felt broken at the end of the meeting but a little closer to being free" (203). Yet in actuality, the balloon was "slowly dying in a tree," a testament to what one might deem the psychological effects of exorcism versus the reality. The release of the balloon causes one's psychological angst to diminish, if not fade, but does not provide true freedom.

For these women, true freedom would entail the erasure of memory, which is impossible. Sophie's fight with the cane stalks, which Rena describes as "confrontational therapy"—may in fact free her enough so that she can sustain a relationship with her husband. According to the therapist, "You will never be able to connect with your husband until you say good-bye to your father" (209). Only by returning to Haiti does Sophie achieve the freedom that her mother needed death to obtain. By running into the cane field and confronting the scene of the rape and the memory of her father, Sophie obtains agency.

The constant reminder that "there are secrets you cannot keep" (85) represents not only the transgressive acts of the women in the novel but also Danticat's transgressive act of writing about these women, their intimate relationships with one another, and the taboo act of mother-daughter incest. As Atie states, "You do not have to name something to make it anymore yours" (134); and although Danticat never names the kinds of transgressive acts that occur, they are part of the Caco family legacy and more broadly inscribed within Haitian culture.

The novel's title, *Breath, Eyes, Memory*, signifies on the meaning of the Haitian oral tradition as it denotes the manner by which stories are aural and captured in the mind's eye through rememory. Danticat shows how the Haitian oral tradition is connected to traditions from Africa, the Caribbean, and America. She articulates various methods of call-and-response that derived from Africa and closely resemble the oral traditions that evolved throughout the diaspora. From the African oral tradition of cry-and-response to the beating of drums and the calls of conch shells, oral traditions serve as the foundation of Haitian cultural expression.

Various examples in the novel exemplify Haitian culture's reliance on call-and-response and its significant role in daily communication. From the traditional greeting cry, "Honneur," and its response, "Respet," call-and-response is used both liberally and distinctly. Grandma Ife's last cry, "Ou Libere?," is used among merchant women as they carry their baskets to and fro. As Danticat writes, "The female street vendors called to one another as they came down the road. When one merchant dropped her heavy basket, another called out of concern, 'Ou libere?' Are you free from your heavy load? The woman with the load would answer yes, if she had unloaded her freight without hurting herself" (96). Sophie never verbally affirms the call for liberation because Grandma Ife silences Sophie's voice. This silence complicates the ending of the novel, raising questions about whether she achieves ultimate freedom. The fact that she has indeed been injured by her traumatic past offers evidence that she will never be free of her burden. The sexual trauma that she endured has produced too many scars, and her mother's death testifies to the effects of trauma on women and to one woman's inability to carry the burden. In the context of Haitian culture, all women must carry burdens, and the manner in which that burden is unloaded constitutes a major concern.

However, the novel suggests that Sophie can only achieve freedom through a communal unloading that transplants the jazz ethos into the Haitian landscape: "There is a place where, if you listen closely in the night, you will hear your mother telling a story and at the end of the tale, she will ask you this question: 'Ou libere? Are you free my daughter?' My grandmother quickly pressed her fingers over my lips. 'Now,' she said, 'you will know how to answer'" (234). Grandma Ife's call is coded, signifying on Sophie's countless burdens: her mother's memory, her traumatic memories of the testing, and most important, the burden of a silenced community of women. Grandma Ife acknowledges that individual assertion remains impossible until one has listened to the group. In listening to the tales that previously have been silenced, the hearer can be free to assume her own identity through voice. Thus, the narrative can free both storyteller and listener. Sophie's freedom lies in the act of narration, as Grandma Ife admonishes: "Listen. Listen before it passes. *Parol gin pie zel*. The words can give wings to your feet" (234). Danticat enables us to hear Sophie's affirmative response to the question of freedom in the loud silence of her jazz narrative.

Transposing the jazz lens onto Danticat's novel allows readers to view the book within the context of a new genre: the Caribbean American jazz novel. By reading the text through the jazz lens, we can understand how the jazz ethos is transplanted onto the Haitian cultural space, cultivating a sense of freedom that enables all the women to answer the communal cry, "Ou libere, are you free?" with affirmative acts of freedom. Reading the novel through a jazz lens enables us to notice the complex fate that Danticat weaves into the cultural fabric of the narrative. Freedom, for the Caco women and more generally Haitian women, lies within their ability to obtain agency in order to revise Old World traditions and create a newly improvised female subject.

Chapter 6

THE FISHER KING AND THE WOMEN OF JAZZ

Paule Marshall's novel *The Fisher King* (2000) is yet another African diasporic novel that emphasizes the complex relationship between jazz and gender. The novel explores the centrality of women's stories as they improvise on language and image. Unlike Marshall's *Brown Girl, Brownstones*, *The Fisher King* weds female-centered cultural narratives with the jazz aesthetic.[1] Jazz haunts the staccato rhythm of Black women's lives as they learn to improvise in order to survive; jazz band dynamics abound as women call and respond to the tension that permeates the culturally diverse community of Bedford-Stuyvesant; and jazz improvisation characterizes the recurring musings of the protagonist Hattie Carmichael, the one "closest" (Marshall 26) to the music of legendary jazz musician Sonny-Rett Payne, the novel's namesake.

Yet, the vital role that women hold throughout the text is absent in any promotional material associated with the novel. In fact, women are excluded from the title and jacket copy of the book:

> In 1949 Sonny-Rett Payne, a black jazz pianist, fled New York for Paris to escape both his family's disapproval of his art and the racism that shadowed his career. . . . Decades after Sonny-Rett left, his eight-year-old Parisian grandson is brought to his old Brooklyn neighborhood to attend a memorial concert in Payne's honor. The child's visit reveals the persistent rivalries within the family and the community that drove his grandfather into exile. Will the young boy be a harbinger of change and reconciliation or a pawn in the power struggle of those who now wish to claim him in Sonny-Rett's name?

This synopsis elides the story's women: Sonny-Rett Payne flees New York with his wife Cherisse, and his lover Hattie soon follows; Hattie brings Sonny-Rett's grandson, Sonny, to Brooklyn. After Hattie and Sonny return to Brooklyn for the concert, we learn that it was only a ruse to entice them back to New York, a development that makes Hattie's homecoming with Sonny central rather than peripheral to the narrative. Through this synopsis, Marshall's jazz novel has been unjustly marketed and often read as a patrilineal text in which Black women's voices constitute a barely audible hum, in contrast to the blaring sounds of the male jazz musician Sonny-Rett Payne. However, a close reading of the novel reveals the audacious voices of the women in the book, particularly Hattie Carmichael's narration of and claim to Sonny-Rett Payne's legacy. Indeed, Hattie becomes the vessel through which Sonny-Rett can be reborn and memorialized. Thus her narrative voice—her "special music"—makes Sonny-Rett's music possible.

Throughout *The Fisher King*, Marshall underscores Hattie's role in Sonny-Rett's life and more broadly the role of women in jazz discourse.[2] Hattie provides a jazz cadence that emphasizes Black women as an integral part of the jazz tradition. She functions as the bass line of the jazz novel, bearing witness to Sonny-Rett's work and translating his success and failures for the community of listeners. In addition, Hattie literally serves as the purveyor of the music, selling jazz records in a music store. Moreover, as a jazz impresario, she manages her own all-girl band as well as Sonny-Rett's career, and she is viewed as the "fathermothersisterbrother" (16) to the music's heir, Sonny. Hattie's significance in Sonny-Rett Payne's life and in the novel broadly testifies to the pivotal role that women played as interlocutors of jazz discourse.

Although recent scholarship on *The Fisher King* acknowledges Hattie, she has yet to be read as the main protagonist who generates the action and ultimately becomes the heroine.[3] A feminist reading of *The Fisher King* focusing on Hattie Carmichael and the novel's other women positions them as the archival entities that pass on the legacy of jazz and ultimately free the music from its structural and gendered boundaries. Marshall literally and figuratively creates a space for Black women to find agency and challenge male-dominated narratives about jazz in the United States and abroad. Marshall constructs

Hattie as an improviser and innovator, thereby placing women at the center of jazz literary discourse. Through a jazz lens that consists of three motifs that recur throughout women's jazz novels—the Wild Woman, the jazz moment of improvisation, and call-and-response—this chapter explores how Marshall employs jazz's essential elements of improvisation and freedom to highlight the significant role that women have played in the creation and development of jazz music, conveying the stories that prevail long after the music has stopped playing. Ultimately, *The Fisher King* becomes a prime example of Marshall's ability to (re)inscribe the interconnections among women, jazz music, and oral tradition.

The Fisher King explores the Wild Woman trope through such characters as Ulene Payne, Florence Varina McCullum-Jones, Cherisse Jones, and Hattie Carmichael. These women continuously, figuratively, and literally improvise on their sexuality, voice, and history in an effort to preserve their dignity and allow them to gain agency. What differentiates these women from other characters is their ability to "cut-and-contrive" (Marshall 99)—that is, to improvise and reconstruct gendered boundaries and thereby reclaim power by challenging the middle-class African American politics of respectability.[4]

The Fisher King begins with Ulene Payne standing at the iron gates, guarding the entrance to her home, in which resides a grand piano that symbolizes jazz music, generations, and tradition. She taught Sonny-Rett how to play classical music through the art of improvisation on this player piano. The iron gates that stand between her and eight-year-old Sonny Carmichael Payne are closed to Hattie when she brings Sonny to visit his great-grandmother. Seen as an outsider, Hattie is not permitted to enter. Despite the silence at the gate, body language speaks volumes—a "cut eye" (15) that lets Hattie know that the older woman wants to be alone with her great-grandson. As soon as Hattie, the interloper, leaves, the gates swing open, and Sonny is allowed access into the home, which "reminded him of the castles and fortresses he was good at drawing" (14). It is not by chance that the gatekeeper in his drawings is male, while in reality he stands before a female. At the outset of the novel, the juxtaposition foreshadows the gendered and generational parallels that are repeated throughout.

Inside, Ulene leads Sonny through her filthy home into a room with a pristine grand piano. Here, Ulene introduces Sonny to his grandfather via photograph and shows him how to play the piano in the same way she taught her son:

> First, she slowly spread his fingers and arched them slightly. This done, she then began guiding his hands to where the keys left and right were sinking down, trying to reach them and place his fingers on as many of them as possible in the fraction of a second before they rose again. For the longest time she repeatedly steered his hands back and forth across the keyboard, showing him how the game was played, while the huge sheet of paper with its hieroglyphics of cuts and nicks scrolled majestically down before his eyes and the music soared. (21)

Ulene takes the position of teacher and mentor. Although the player piano is playing classical music, Sonny's hand movements are improvised and in the tradition of stride piano. Improvisation for Ulene is not limited to teachings on the player piano; it becomes her way of life as she learns how to "cut-and-contrive" to survive in America.

Traveling on the SS *Nerissa*, Ulene made her way to New York with her friend, Alva, "with nothing but a gripsack and two willing hands" (97). She took on work cleaning homes on Long Island and taking care of other people's children until she married Bertram Payne and had two kids of her own (98). But then her husband died suddenly:

> [Bertram was] never sick a day in his life and then one night in his sleep a stroke. They said it was a stroke. You wake the morning to find the man dead next to you in bed. And the house on Macon Street the two of you just start to buy to be paid for, the mortgage they had to get from the loan shark when the banks refuse them being they was Colored, higher—three, four time higher—than any bank's. And two boychildren to raise her one. And times hard after that idiot Hoover nearruined the country. Rich people turned poor overnight throwing themselves out the windows cause they don't know how to cut-and-contrive. That's what you must do, y'know, when times

is hard. Is what she, Ulene Agatha Payne, born Cummings, Mis'
Cummings' girlchild, did right away: cut-and-contrive. (99)

Simply put, to cut-and-contrive is to improvise. Ulene thus learns
the art of improvisation to make a life for herself and her children.
As musicologist Paul Berliner writes, improvisers "perpetually make
split-second decisions about suitable materials and their treatment"
(Berliner 497). These split-second decisions are rooted in memory,
characterized by deliberate spontaneity, and replete with creative
possibilities that transcend the musical score. Ulene demonstrates
the art of cutting-and-contriving in three instances. First, she literally cuts her home into multiple spaces by constructing rooms for
boarders. Second, she returns to working for white people. Third,
she sells handed-down gifts to earn money. She does these things to
"meet the loan shark mortgage each month and to pay for Everett's
lessons." For Ulene, "it was cut-and-contrive down to the very toilet
paper" (Marshall 100).

Ulene was not the only woman who had to learn how to improvise a living to remain financially intact: "West Indian and American alike—everybody catching it but a hundred times worse if you
black—crowd together, sheltering from the rain, hot sun, and snow
under the stairs to the El at Albemarle Road and waiting to dash out
in the road the minute a car with a Madame at the wheel start to pull
over" (99). Ulene and many other women in the community, including Florence Varina McCullum-Jones, had to improvise to meet the
financial demands of running a single-parent household. Despite the
fact that she is of a different culture and socioeconomic standing from
Ulene, Florence Varina, too, becomes financially unable to sustain her
living, though in her case it is because of divorce rather than death.
As Ulene remarks, "The foolish woman din' know it but she was gon
have to learn how to cut-and-contrive" (100).

Florence Varina indeed learns to cut-and-contrive, by convincing
the Conservancy to acknowledge her home as a historic site. After
she is humiliated by an employer who demands that she wears the
same colored bow as the dog she has been asked to walk, Florence
becomes determined to ensure that her daughter, Cherisse, can continue "the singing, dance and acting lessons" that could make her

into a modern-day Lena Horne (119). After chancing upon a brochure for the "Landmark Conservancy Tours, Brooklyn Chapter," Florence "appeared at the Conservancy office downtown Brooklyn armed with pictures of the full grown Magnolia Grandiflora in her front yard. She also brought the family bible with its date of birth entered in Gayton McCullum's hand and proceeded to tell the story of how it came to be. . . . Florence Varina talking for dear life" (120). In Marshall's novel, language rather than music serves as what Kenneth Burke calls "equipment for living" (Burke 593). Yet like music, language can be fluid and achieve the improvisatory qualities inherent in jazz. The solemn story about her father's journey from the South to the North that Florence Varina delivers for the weekly tour can be read as neither fact nor fiction but rather as improvisation.

Traveling with her father from the South, "Miss Grandiflora," as Florence Varina calls the tree planted by her father that has been growing in her backyard since April 9, 1889, represents both tenacity and rootedness and serves as a reminder of the Great Migration. Miss G. also remains a symbol of longevity for the African American community, which felt displaced but nevertheless survived in the North. Intertwined with this tree's branches, Florence Varina is the first Mc-Cullum child to be born in the North. Thus, her name appears in the family Bible after that of Miss G., whom Florence describes as the "real tree that grows in Brooklyn" (Marshall 113). Florence Varina McCullum is named after a piece of land—more specifically, "the only county in Georgia at the time where Colored were allowed to own land" (115). Florence Varina muses that her father "went and put Varina in [her] name. As another reminder, I guess, along with Miss G., of the one place on God's earth where he'd once had his own land" (120). Thus, freedom is inherent in Florence Varina's name, and this freedom emerges in her improvisatory style. She uses Miss G. to maintain that freedom as financial security through her improvisation with the Conservancy tour.

Others in the novel recognize Florence Varina and her mastery of improvisation, highlighting the centrality of cut-and-contrive to women's lives. When Sonny brings a branch of the tree into Ulene's home, she admits that Florence takes the prize for knowing how to cut-and-contrive:

Come marching in here with part of some old tree that [Florence] been fooling the public with for years, claiming it's a tree her father planted all the way back when God said "Come, let us make trees," and that her father—he must have been an obeah man—was the only body to get it to grow 'cause it wasn't suited to the weather up here. All of it nothing but some who-struck-john story. But I know she got people to believe her. Every week you see a van pulling up to the house. Foolish people paying good money to come see it and to hear the who-struck-john story. I tell yuh, I have to hand it to her. I thought I knew how to cut-and-contrive to keep going, but old-miss-young walks away with the prize. (Marshall 170)

Florence Varina's ability to construct the "personal story" of Miss G.'s voyage from the South to the North can be read as a performance filled with improvised language and images from the beginning of her story, where she evokes jazz by comparing herself to "that Duke Ellington song: 'Don't Get Around Much Anymore'" (113), to the "theatrical pauses" (117), and finally to the props such as the Bible and the wax fruit that looked like a "grenade" (120). Florence's weekly story becomes a performance, and she, with her "russet-dyed hair, her cover girl makeup, her earrings and choker and the even more elaborate at-home gown, almost a ball gown . . . a pair of high-heeled mules in the same fabric as the gown" (112), becomes like Lena Horne—the embodiment of her dreams for Cherisse.

Expanding the branches of the family tree, Cherisse is known for her "Shirley Temple curls" and for her singing ambitions, and many, particularly young Hattie, envy her: "sometimes peering at the tableau inside 258 from the hunter's blind provided her by the darkness, the longing Hattie felt would become so acute, so filled with anger she would want to rush inside, yank the show-off out of her chair, chase her from the dining room, from the house, from Macon Street even, just dispossess her utterly and install herself at the family table" (69).

However, rather than replacing Cherisse, Hattie becomes her friend—so close, in fact, that in junior high school they were kissing friends, the "kind of friends that prompted the other kids to say: 'If you sees one, you know you gots to see the other!'" (69). Hattie and

Cherisse are described as one, "Hattie losing her ordinary-looking self and becoming with each deep kiss and caress the much-loved, dressed-up, prized daughter at the dining room table" (70). Further, as an adult, Hattie gathers Cherisse and three other women to begin an all-girl group, the Maconettes.

Cherisse thus becomes the object not only of Hattie's gaze but also that of the audience. Although Cherisse's stardom is short-lived, her desire to be wanted or the object of the gaze never ceases: "Cherisse behaved at times as if she was actually on the bandstand performing with [Sonny-Rett] and the trio or the band. Because when a tune ended and the applause rose, she would often, without being aware of it, bow her head ever so slightly and smile, appropriating part or perhaps all of the applause for herself in acknowledgment of her perfect limbs, perfect breasts, and the milk chocolate perfection of her face" (183). Sonny-Rett remarks approvingly, "Being admired is far more important to [Cherisse] than love any day" (183). Both Hattie and Cherisse embody improvisation through a marked fluidity of their sexual identities. Cherisse explores her desire for admiration by engaging in intimate relationships with both her husband and Hattie. Hattie recalls that Cherisse used a French term: "*Partager* it's the verb to share . . . then she smiled wickedly and kissed her on either cheek" (192). The three were inseparable, "a flesh and blood triangle" with Hattie serving as the "base that connects the two" (184).

Although both Hattie and Cherisse exhibit fluid sexualities, Hattie's resistance to the boundaries associated with gender norms and other power structures that restrain her socially, culturally, and sexually marks her as the quintessential Wild Woman, from her improvised sexuality to her spontaneous performances. Hattie's sexual relationship with Cherisse continues until Cherisse dies of cancer: "Up to the end she nursed her all day, and sometimes on the nights when she didn't work, Hattie held her—a mere wraith—in the bed and ever so gently loved her as when they were girls practicing their kissing and touching upstairs at Mis' Dawson's, reassuring her gift of a best friend that she would always possess the power to draw every eye in a room to her perfect self" (206).

Hattie's sexual relationship with Sonny-Rett is quite the opposite, not about becoming one but about power dynamics:

When he was ready, she slowly drew him into her wonderfully complicated, inexplicable self, proving to him, as she did each time they were together, that even an ordinary, unremarkable body such as hers possessed a kind of music, its own rhythms, harmonies, tonalities, crescendos—more than one, and that, at times, her special music had the power to leave him in tears afterward on her breast. Pleasure that great. (193)

Here, Hattie remains in full control of Sonny and holds the ability to become the object of his gaze. She is attempting to make him hear her body's "special music." And Hattie's power is not limited to the realm of physical interaction but also exists in the oral sphere. More than any other quality, Hattie's ability to use language grants her agency and enables her to enter the jazz discourse through her jazz moment.

Characterized by a pattern of fragmentation, reconfiguration, and assertion, the jazz moment is ultimately a moment of improvisation—sudden, unexpected, yet calculated, since the jazz figure experiencing the moment has prepared for it all throughout their life. The protagonist reconfigures these memories into the reality of the moment and improvises within that moment. The improvisational moment, a moment of assertion, occurs in the break between memory and present reality.

Hattie has spent years preparing for this moment. Sonny-Rett's brother, Edward Payne, writes to Hattie to request her attendance at the memorial concert, highlighting her relationship to Sonny, which is outsung only by her relationship to the music itself: "You were the one closest to my brother's work from the beginning and you, more than anyone else, including the critics, understood what he was attempting to do and say with his music" (26). As a jazz pianist in the 1940s, Sonny-Rett created a "new kind of music" (137) that can be associated with the bebop era, and Hattie's singular ability to understand what Sonny was saying with his music testifies to her intimate knowledge of both the artist and his music. From her work at the record shop to her countless conversations with Sonny-Rett and her relationship with him as lover and manager, she is more than prepared to give a full account of his life by translating his music into language.

Marshall constructs Hattie as a figure who represents jazz, and her jazz moment of improvisation is written into the narrative as a complex event that enables readers to understand the life stories behind the music. Hattie's jazz moment is captured within a symphonic rendering of the music that alludes to the breaks, solos, and improvisation that defined jazz in the late 1940s. Yet the life stories are told through a female lens, thereby establishing the Black woman as an archival body for jazz, history, and memory.

Hattie's jazz moment of improvisation happens through a series of vignettes that are in dialogue with the music. The vignettes, told in a doubling manner, preface Sonny-Rett's seven hit recordings. She speaks words aloud for the audience to hear, while some stories remain personal memories. Thus, even as she is onstage during the memorial concert, Hattie pursues "a counterpoint of other memories that were not for the public's ear as she spoke" (183). The ambiguity between the spoken and the unspoken allows the tension to rise and fall through the music and in the narrative. The story seems ultimately layered like jazz—what is spoken aloud is only the tip of the iceberg, with much more hidden beneath the surface. We ultimately learn that every tune Sonny-Rett ever played was a song about his life, echoing Amiri Baraka's contention that "the song and the people is the same" (*Blues People* 191) and that the people convey their stories through the music—in this case, both literally and figuratively. Most significant here are the performance aspects, in which Hattie must embody the music and become the bearer of much more than Sonny-Rett's life. Hattie becomes a part of the band, much like a female vocalist, and must learn how to play with and against the band by mastering the art of call-and-response.

The concert begins with "Sonny-Rett plays Sonny" and "Basically Bach, Basically Blue," both the hits for which he was most famous. The music is followed by a memory from Hattie: "Once applause died, Hattie had stepped to the lectern, the stage lights over the band had dimmed and a single bright cone of light came to focus on her as she opened the folder containing her notes" (Marshall 181). The lights, bright over her head and dimmed over the band, suggest that she will perform the solo. When Hattie steps to the lectern, the oral tradition is suffused into the musical break.

Hattie's narrative fills each break between the musical selections. Her solo is further identified on the page with a literal symbol that distinguishes her private memory and the life stories heard by the audience. Within these narrative breaks that are not spoken aloud, we are privy to Hattie's identity and the truth behind her relationship with Sonny-Rett, Cherisse, and ultimately the jazz tradition. The entire memorial concert can be read through the lens of Gustav Freytag's narrative pyramid (exposition, rising action, climax, falling action, denouement), thus merging the literary and musical aspects of the text.

In the first break (the exposition), we find the reprise of "that Sunday in '47 when Everett Carlyle Payne was given a chance to sit in with the house band and what happened within these very same walls when he finished putting a hurtin' on the hokey doke tune" (182). Hattie's private thoughts, found in her "counterpoint" solo, introduce the supportive role that she and Cherisse played in Sonny-Rett's life while he climbed the ladder of success: "Whenever he played, she and Cherisse were there also" (183). Hattie disbanded her all-girl group, the Maconettes, after Cherisse lost interest and chose a life with Sonny-Rett. Both women were "seated as close as possible to the bandstand" (183) wherever he played. Hattie was there to give him her opinion— "the only one that mattered"—and Cherisse was there with the "milk chocolate perfection of her face" (183) as a spectacle. In the break, we also learn that the three of them were "inseparable" (184). At this moment in 1946, Hattie's identity was defined in relation to Sonny-Rett. Hattie was his mentor and manager, "handling [his] affairs while he was still local, negotiating the terms of the many little gigs that came his way, seeing to it that he got to the night club on the right night at the right time, and looking after the money for him. That above else" (184). In this moment in the break, Sonny-Rett's identity is defined in relation to Hattie.

As she recalls these memories in the narrative breaks, she is still "recounting the public saga" (185) to the audience. Thus, the private and public memories intertwine with musical titles to create a lyrical medley of Hattie's life with Sonny-Rett and Cherisse. When Hattie mentions "Basically Bach, Basically Blue," the public narrative tells us that "Europe came calling," and she goes on to describe the various invitations Sonny-Rett received to play at international jazz festivals and his eagerness to find a place where he could "breathe and create without a lot of hassle" (185). In her private memory, she delves deeper into the underlying meaning of *hassle* as she describes the racism he endured in the South as well as the North. Thus "Basically Bach, Basically Blue" speaks to the jazz musician's dilemma in the late 1940s, when even famous and wealthy African Americans still suffered under Jim Crow laws and at the hands of the Ku Klux Klan.

In the next narrative break, Hattie introduces Sonny-Rett's two major hits in Europe, "The Crossing" and "Euphoria," which can be read as the rising action both in terms of her narrative about Sonny's life and within the compositional arrangement of the memorial concert. The fine line between her personal and public memories remains intact. "The Crossing" provides the background for her private memory about her communication with Cherisse through letters, which included postscripts from Sonny-Rett encouraging her to come to Europe. By the time the band finishes "Euphoria," we discover that Hattie indeed traveled to Europe, and she, Cherisse, and Sonny-Rett were happier than ever, the "triangle intact again" (189). Hattie "expanded on the theme of the tune" (189) as she discusses publicly the rise of jazz in Europe as a euphoric experience. Hattie moves back and forth from the lectern to her chair, portraying both the public and private memories of the next three compositions, "4th Century BC Stomp," "In the Upper Room," and "Ptite Jojo" (the climax). Her public memory of being on the road with Sonny-Rett juxtaposes with her private memory of an intimate relationship with him and her giving birth to the idea of a baby. The intermission within the narrative also serves as a literal break, with an entirely new chapter starting afterward.

Marshall then introduces more tunes: "Continental Free Fall," "Sodom and Gomorrah Days and Nights," and "Sonny-Rett Plays Sonny . . . Reprise" (199). A distinct change occurs in Hattie's tone: "She began speaking this time in a surprisingly flat, factual, voice about the jazz scene in Europe, how it started to change around the mid-sixties, especially in France" (200). This shift not only signals the falling action, but calls our attention to what is being said. Hattie, for the first time, riffs on the period and inserts herself as a subject to explain that jazz was replaced by "a whole lotta noise that the white boys playing it had the nerve to call Rock and Roll and even Rhythm and Blues. Stealing our stuff" (200). Before ending her public discourse, she tells the members of the audience that they can hear "the long free-fall" in Sonny-Rett's final compositions, "Continental Free Fall" and "Sodom and Gomorrah Days and Nights" (201). Hattie then closes the "folder with her notes (she had scarcely consulted them all evening) and return[s] to her seat" (201). This last line before we enter her personal memory posits Hattie as an improviser. Although the notes are in front of her, she knows the life story behind the music by heart, not just because she understood Sonny-Rett personally but because his life story was hers. Hattie's jazz moment inscribes her own story into the conventional narrative of a once-famous jazz musician. The literal breaks found throughout the memorial concert dedicated to Hattie's personal memory create jazz moments that define her identity, provide her with agency, and inscribe her personal story as part of the life stories behind the music.

At the end of Hattie's personal narrative, we encounter "Sonny-Rett Plays Sonny . . . Reprise" (199), which can be read as the denouement. The Tin Pan Alley tune, transformed again but this time into a "tender, complex, and eloquent New Orleans processional dirge out to the burial ground. His tenor, with its natural sweetness, not only bringing home Sonny-Rett Payne, born Everett Carlyle, Ulene's boy-child, but also bidding him a respectful and loving farewell, putting him to rest properly on native ground" (209). Thus, by the end of the memorial concert, Sonny-Rett is buried within the proper national and matrilineal context.

In one of the most telling jazz scenes in *The Fisher King*, Hattie Carmichael relates the tale about how Everett Carlyle Payne became Sonny-Rett Payne:

> It was the first time he got a chance to sit in with the band. . . . Something Abe Kaiser had started called Sunday Jazz at the Putnam Royal. And of all things, he decided to play some hokey-doke, Tin Pan Alley tune called "Sonny Boy Blue." . . . [F]rom the very first chord it was "Sonny Boy Blue" like it had never been played before. . . . That tune . . . didn't have nothing to do with Tin Pan Alley or Broadway when he laid into it. Nobody

we knew, certainly nobody from Brooklyn had ever played piano like that. . . . We couldn't believe what we were hearing. . . .
Sat there . . . like we were in church and weren't supposed to
clap. Everybody Spellbound. . . . Until Alvin jumped up all of a
sudden and started shouting "Sonny-Rett! Sonny-Rett! Sonny
Rett!" And pointing to him up on the bandstand with the hand
he had left. . . . Your brother took that sappy little tune, put a
hurtin' on it like Shades said, and made it his tune, his song,
Alvin understood that and made it part of his name. (80)

In this passage, the narrative perspective is gendered female since we
follow Sonny's rebirth through Hattie's eyes. The passage demonstrates
the breadth and depth of Hattie's knowledge about jazz music, including different musical periods and chord changes. Hattie describes the
crowd as silent, dumbfounded by Sonny-Rett's musical composition.
In his jazz moment of improvisation, Sonny-Rett takes a tune and
makes it his own. His new name and new identity combine the blues
and his new way of playing jazz. The passage not only renames Everett Payne, but also extends the jazz tradition to include a female
voice that knows the music well enough to translate and transcend
its social, structural, and gendered boundaries. In her jazz moment,
Hattie takes the narrative of Sonny-Rett's genesis and makes it
her own.

The song that prompts both Sonny-Rett's and Hattie's jazz moments echoes James Baldwin's jazz short story, "Sonny's Blues" (1957),
and Marshall responds to Baldwin's call by presenting a narrative
that highlights rather than obscures the female voice. Scholar Robert B. Stepto's call-and-response theory can help explore further
Marshall's jazz novel as a response to the literary call for Black
women improvisers in jazz literature. While both Sonny-Rett Payne
and Baldwin's Sonny are affected by jazz music, Baldwin's narrative fails to underscore the depth to which women were involved
in the jazz musician's life. Baldwin's story is told through the male
perspective (via Sonny's brother), whereas in Marshall's text, Sonny-
Rett's brother relinquishes all authority to a woman. Although both
Baldwin and Marshall set their narratives during the heyday of jazz
and the bebop era, Baldwin chooses Harlem as his main setting,

while Marshall extends our understanding of the place and space of the music by locating her characters in Brooklyn, a lesser-known but equally productive locale for jazz music. The life and music of Sonny-Rett Payne not only echo "Sonny's Blues," but also extend the boundaries of that story by narrating it through the Black female voice and highlighting the Black female as improviser and innovator in tandem with the male improviser.

If Baldwin depicts the absence of family within "Sonny's Blues" (in which both Sonny and his father lose brothers to interracial violence), Marshall reconstructs the family in a complex way by defining Hattie Carmichael as "fathermothersisterbrother" (16). Marshall ultimately positions a magnifying lens on the silenced portions of Baldwin's jazz short story and re-creates a narrative that depicts not only why Sonny experienced his (down)fall but also how and who bears responsibility. Further, Marshall expounds on other parts of Baldwin's narrative, such as the international reach of the music, by recounting the story through a transnational lens. Finally, Marshall revises the narrative time span of the music. Rather than relegate the story to the late 1940s, she pushes it into the 1970s to describe the music's longevity through generations of Black women.

The narrative organization of *The Fisher King* can be viewed through the lens of a jazz performance—what anthropologist John Szwed calls the "musical social organization" of jazz:

Jazz has a distinctive musical social organization in performance. Jazz musicians play against as well as with other jazz musicians, working one rhythm or melody against another competitively but also reciprocally. It's what Ralph Ellison called the cruel contradiction implicit in the music, the individual finding personal identity against and with the group. Individual musicians assert themselves in solos, but other musicians may enter into each other's solos, not so much as an interruption but as a gesture of support and attentiveness. Jazz at its most complex—say, during collectively improvised playing—calls on the musicians to play with unique voices, to sound like no one else, and yet at the same time to cohere as one, with a single goal. (56–57)

The musical organization of jazz serves as a metaphor for the narrative construction of Marshall's text. For Ellison, antagonistic cooperation is defined as playing with and against the group, simultaneously occupying a space as an individual and as part of the collective. An individual may survive on and because of "shit, grit, and mother wit" (Ellison 176), but that individual's being always exists in relation to others, especially as with regard to jazz group dynamics. Moreover, jazz musicians are encouraged to "tell the story," and that ability is central to *The Fisher King* narrative, as Hattie riffs on the improvised oral narrative of the life stories behind the music. All of the women in the novel amplify their own melodies or voices to convey their stories of love, family, and loss. These stories directly relate to the underlining narrative rhythm of the jazz tradition.

Examining Marshall's novel through a jazz lens enables readers to view the text within the confines of a new genre, the African diasporic jazz novel. The jazz ethos is transplanted onto a cultural space, thereby placing all the women in the text into jazz discourse through their individual stories. Reading the novel through a jazz lens also allows us to see how the life stories behind the music engage a community of women. The jazz lens provides a sense of innovation and possibility for the female subject to obtain agency and identity by redefining jazz discourse through untold life stories.

Marshall claims the übermasculine jazz tradition by resisting the boundaries of culture and enables Hattie to improvise an identity within that framework to create "her special music." That jazz plays such a significant role in the novel for Hattie demonstrates not only jazz's malleability but also Marshall's creativity, transforming the novel into a revisionist narrative that responds to the call of the absent Black female voice in jazz literature. Ultimately, Marshall affirms that modern jazz possesses an obscured femininity and a diasporic cultural identity that have yet to enter the discourse.

TOWARD A WOMANIST JAZZ LENS

Gender and Jazz in Poetry and Dance

Like the classic blues tradition of the 1920s, modern African diaspora literature becomes a jazz space where Black women can find agency and freedom in image, language, and action. Throughout the literary texts examined in this book, we notice how the confluence of gender and jazz creates the trope of the Wild Woman figure, coded dialogue in the form of cry-and-response and improvisational acts of resistance by Black women. Further, this tripartite trope also applies to other fields of study that combine jazz and gender. In this brief conclusion, I would like to examine how the tripartite womanist jazz trope can be useful in examining Duke Ellington's *A Drum Is a Woman*, the performance poetry of Jayne Cortez, and the movements of jazz dancer Carmen de Lavallade.

Alice Walker offers a multilayered meaning of womanism and distinguishes it from feminism in that "Womanist is to feminist as purple is to lavender." The distinction seems to suggest that Black women's struggles are deeper as they lie at the intersection of race, gender, and class. Walker's extensive definition of womanist can be found in her seminal text *In Search of Our Mothers' Gardens: Womanist Prose*. Walker defines the term womanist as:

> From *womanish*. (Opp. of "girlish," i.e. frivolous, irresponsible, not serious.) A Black feminist or feminist of color. From the Black folk expression of mothers to female children, "you acting womanish," i.e., like a woman. Usually referring to outrageous, audacious, courageous or *willful* behavior. Wanting to know more and in greater depth than is considered "good" for one. Interested in grown up doings. Acting grown up. Being

grown up. Interchangeable with another Black folk expression: "You trying to be grown." Responsible. In charge. *Serious.* (Walker 45)[1]

Walker's definition fully encapsulates the nuances ascribed to a reading of Black womanhood in jazz texts. A womanist reading sharpens our focus on the role of Black women in the über-masculine discourse of jazz and on jazz music's possibilities for freedom, within a Black feminist matrix of respectability politics. The jazz lens and its tripartite focus on Wild Women improvisation, and call-and-response can also be useful for analyzing the relationship between Black women and jazz beyond the literary novel. I would like to return to Duke Ellington's *A Drum Is a Woman* and discuss the importance of reading the allegory through a womanist framework. Let us examine how the womanist framework applies to Ellington's album through Margaret Tyne's jazz vocals, Carmen de Lavallade's jazz dance, and Jayne Cortez's jazz poetry. While these texts might differ in genre, they are similar in their use of the jazz aesthetic to create and empower Black female subjectivity.

Ellington's *A Drum Is a Woman* begins with the beautifully haunting soprano voice of opera singer Margaret Tyne as she delivers the first line, "a drum is a woman who won't stay out of your blood." Tyne's voice is buttressed by the staccato rhythms of Ellington's piano and the rhythmic drums from the orchestra. However, like a phantom, Tyne cannot be seen, she can only be heard singing "a drum is a woman who haunts you all day long." Tyne's voice is also disembodied as dancer Carmen de Lavallade adopts it through her character portrayal of Madam Zajj (whose name is a play on the word Jazz). *A Drum* tells the story of Madam Zajj's journey throughout the world with Carribee Joe, as she portrays the history of the jazz tradition. Madam Zajj becomes the vehicle used to gain knowledge about the history of the music. Scholars have suggested that Ellington's album can be seen as an allegory, which declares jazz's journey from its origins in Africa to America and recognizes its development in spirituals, blues, and bebop. While the allegory seems to imply that the drum represents jazz music's journey through space and over time, many have failed to remark upon how a womanist reading of the drum's journey would consider the personification of the drum as a Black female subject significant.

By way of personification, we can read the drum's journey and Madam Zajj's as one in the same, as developing within the jazz tradition. Through a womanist reading of the narrative lyrics as well as the visual moments from the television series, we can follow not only the transnational journey of jazz's development but also the development of the Black female subject from object of denigration to subject of improvisation. "A drum" depicts the Black female journey as complicated moments filled with irony and contradictions. Madam Zajj becomes empowered to travel the world and is both honored and revered; yet as a drum, she is also abused, objectified, and played by all. Thus, *A Drum* can be seen as the first jazz album to present the nuances of Black womanhood in language and image. It is this complex journey of the performance of Black female subjectivity and its relationship to the jazz tradition that best characterizes Ellington's album. De Lavallade's sweeping dance performance as Madam Zajj redefines Black female subjectivity as limitless, demonstrating Black women's freedom in language, image, and moments of improvisation.

Madam Zajj adopts language and dance to express her desires. Throughout the US Steel Hour television program, Madam Zajj speaks infrequently as her story is told through the narrative voice of Duke Ellington; however, when she does speak or channel Margaret Tyne's voice, it is a call expressing her longing for Carribee Joe. The first time she comes to voice is after the Mardi Gras parade scene.[2] Ellington's narrative voice asks Madam Zajj "How does it feel to be first lady of Mardi Gras?" Madam Zajj responds, "I'm beat and blue for Joe." Then she performs a solo dance, "Carribee Joe Part I." Madam Zajj's body becomes the central focus of the camera as her legs glide and her arms flail. The power of her dance is like language calling and responding to her own beat. According to scholar Thomas DeFrantz, "all African diaspora dance, including black social dances, may be likened to verbal language most in its conspicuous employment of 'call and response' with the body responding to and provoking the voice of the drum" (DeFrantz 66). Ultimately, Madam Zajj's dancing summons Carribee Joe and they are reunited in Congo Square. The power of her dance is exacting, as it becomes a language that communicates her desires. Madam Zajj is capable of attaining her desires through not only movement on the dance stage but also movement through space. Madam Zajj's flying image throughout the US Steel Hour show underscores her potential for transnational freedom. Madam Zajj's image at various intervals throughout the hour positions her in the sky, among the clouds, flying from Africa to Barbados, New Orleans, Chicago, The World, The Moon, and New York City. The theme of flying casts Madam Zajj as counternarrative to the legend of the flying African. Scholar Nassourou Imorou describes the legend as "a canonical tale, which resonates throughout the expressive traditions of that part of the African Diaspora which has known slavery in the New World" (Imorou 48). Thus the image of Madam Zajj flying situates her within African diasporic folklore and connotes her ability to escape oppressive situations. The flying theme is also representative of her ability to improvise. Like the other Wild Women found throughout the book, the ability to improvise is significant as it can mean life or death (literally and symbolically).

Madam Zajj's act of improvisation is seen throughout the television series as she disappears and reappears at will. Her transformation from a drum to a woman and back to a drum suggests a fluid identity. Madam Zajj cannot be contained literally or within gender-specific boundaries. Scholar Shane Vogel describes Zajj's fluid identity as a "transnational, transgendered, transhuman body that stands in for the (philosophy of the) history of jazz, which is itself a history of the production of subjectivities in-resistance" (Vogel 130). As a figure in resistance, Madam Zajj can be seen as a wild woman par excellence, using dance and language to trace a limitless Black female subjectivity.

This idealization of Black female subjectivity is challenged by the reality of Black women's lives in Jayne Cortez's poem "If the Drum Is a Woman." Cortez's poetry is deeply rooted in the jazz aesthetic. Her poem "If the Drum Is a Woman" responds to Ellington's jazz album by referencing the historical violence and mistreatment against Black women. Unlike Ellington's album, the Black female subject in Cortez's poem is not free, nor does she have agency. Instead, she is marginalized, abused, raped, and beaten. However, Cortez's acts of improvisational resistance can be found throughout her jazz poetry.

Similar to the jazz-like qualities of a drum, Cortez's poem is steeped in the blues tradition. According to scholar Tony Bolden, "as is typical in the blues tradition, Cortez appropriates Ellington's music as a basis of improvisation for her own tune in order to foreground gender violence" (Bolden 67). Further, the spoken word poem seems to improvise on the AAB blues song form when the poem is recited rather than heard. Each time Cortez repeats the refrain "if" it produces a new stanza. In the first stanza, the poem is questioning the reasons for the rape and physical abuse of Black women. Narratively, Cortez's language shows the irony of likening a woman to a drum. The poem begins with the "if" clause, which suggests a conditional statement that can only be true if the conclusion is true. The "if clause" also suggests that the poem is a response to a prior clause. In this case, Cortez is directly addressing Ellington and men in general who objectify women.

Cortez's spoken word poem delivers a searing critique of men and their abuse of women, Black women specifically. The trope of the Wild Woman is embodied in her rhythmic speech as she liberates poetry from the confines of the page and liberates her voice. Her band, the Firespitters, play in the background and allow for the drums to take center stage. As the drumbeat calls and responds to Cortez's personified reflections on women, language and music come together in moments of improvised synchronization. Cortez seems to be representative of the Wild Women found throughout the book as she pushes the boundaries of language and music, metaphor and reality, to gain ultimate freedom of expression.

In her spoken word performance, Cortez's rhetorical questions are fired into the void of the drumbeat. She questions why an object such as the drum is more revered and respected than the Black female subject that it personifies. The first stanza is describing various levels of physical violence inflicted onto women from "pounding your drum" to "pistol whipping your drum" and finally to "shooting your drum." The escalation of violence serves as a marker of improvisation as it demonstrates the many ways that violence can be enacted. Her lyrics seem like sharp tools as she wields each refrain against the backdrop of jazz music: "Don't beat your drum, don't beat, your drum." The lyrics can be read as both literal and symbolic. This text can be interpreted as

Cortez responding to Duke Ellington's TV program where women are objectified. In defense of the wild woman, Cortez seeks to deconstruct Ellington's metaphor and demonstrate the severe reality of abuse undergone by Black women during this period. Cortez questions, "If the drum is a woman, why do you beat your drum . . . and make drum tragedies out of your drum?" The rhetorical questioning throughout the piece can also be deemed a call to action as it responds to the societal mistreatment of Black women, and women overall.

Cortez goes further in the second stanza to describe how colonization affects the abuser as well as the abused: "But if the drum is a woman / why are you choking your drum / why are you raping your drum?" The poem foregrounds the abuse within the historical context of colonization: "the night is full of displaced persons," the psyche of the abused "bitterness embedded in the flesh"; however, there is hope for peace in the line "this is America and chicken are coming home to roost on the MX missile." This stanza repeats the questioning that occurs in the first stanza, yet with a difference. In the beginning of the stanza, Cortez personalizes the stanza by inserting the subject "I," thereby demonstrating a connection to the oppressor she admonishes. Thereafter, the questioning begins again, yet this time the drum is personalized "your" and personified "mother drum your sister drum your wife drum and your infant daughter drum." This difference suggests the evolution of the drum from object of denigration to subject of denigration. The last stanza consists of a series of counternarratives about Black female identity: "your drum is not docile, your drum is not invisible, your drum is not inferior to you." These counternarratives seem to establish Black female subjectivity. Thereafter she delivers a series of admonishments and a concluding stanza that aims to teach others about the nuances of Black female subjectivity:

If the drum is a woman
then understand your drum . . .
so don't reject your drum don't try to dominate your drum
don't become weak and cold and desert your drum

The final lines of repetition underscore the importance of not abusing Black women. The three types of abuse that this last line seems to represent are physical, emotional, and psychological. Abuse takes many forms, and certainly Cortez is attempting to show through language and music that the kind of abuse she is attempting to correct is neglect. By discussing Black female subjectivity and moving it from the margins of discourse, Cortez's poem centers Black womanhood and demonstrates its significance for the womanist jazz poetry she constructs.

A womanist reading champions the jazz tradition while extending its canon to include Black female improvisation by means of individual assertion, Black women's notion of democratic ideals via jazz band dynamics, and Black women's attainment of freedom within moments of improvisation. Furthermore, by examining the three tropes that comprise the jazz lens, we notice the transformation of the blues woman, created within the classic blues tradition, into the jazz tradition's Wild Woman who responds by echoing the resounding call for Black female subjectivity. Ultimately, the womanist jazz lens enables readers to regard Black women as improvisers/creators/innovators and active participants in jazz discourse.

NOTES

INTRODUCTION: A NEW BEAT, GENERATIONS LATER:
MODERN JAZZ AND AFRICAN DIASPORA WOMEN'S WRITING

1. See John Wriggle's essay, "The Other of All Albums": Revisiting Ellington's
A Drum Is a Woman" in *Duke Ellington Studies*, ed. John Howland (New York:
Cambridge University Press, 2017).

2. Here I am referring to the politics of respectability established around the
turn of the twentieth century by black women of the upper middle class. See
Evelyn Brooks Higginbotham, *Righteous Discontent: The Women's Movement in
the Black Baptist Church, 1880–1920* (Cambridge, MA: Harvard University Press,
1993).

3. See Farah Griffin, "It Takes Two People to Confirm the Truth: The Jazz Fiction
of Sherley Ann Williams and Toni Cade Bambara," in *Big Ears: Listening for Gender
in Jazz Studies*, ed. Nichole T. Rustin and Sherrie Tucker (Durham, NC: Duke
University Press, 2008).

4. Sherrie Tucker, "Where the Blues and the Truth Lay Hiding: Rememory of
Jazz in Black Women's Fiction," *Frontiers: A Journal of Women Studies* 13, no. 2
(1993): 26–44.

5. Griffin, "It Takes Two People to Confirm the Truth."

6. Robert O'Meally, *The Jazz Cadence of American Culture* (New York: Columbia
University Press, 2004).

7. Hazel Carby, "It Jus Be's Dat Way Sometimes: The Sexual Politics of Women's
Blues," in *The Jazz Cadence of American Culture*, ed. Robert O'Meally (New York:
Columbia University Press, 2004).

8. According to Ralph Ellison, "jazz is an art of individual assertion" and the
"true jazz moment is as distinct from the uninspired commercial performance:
spring[ing] from a contest in which each artist challenges all the rest, each solo
flight, or improvisation, represents (like the successive canvases of a painter) a
definition of his identity: as individual, as member of the collectivity, as a link in

the chain of tradition." See Ralph Ellison, *Shadow and Act* (New York: Random House, 1964).

1. REUNITED: (RE)CLAIMING GENDER IN JAZZ NARRATIVES FROM BALDWIN'S "SONNY'S BLUES" TO ANGELOU'S "REUNION"

1. Cheryl Wall, *Worrying the Line: Black Women Writers, Lineage, and Literary Tradition* (Chapel Hill: University of North Carolina Press, 2005).

2. For a detailed discussion of the jazz-literature correspondence, see *The Jazz Cadence of American Culture*, ed. Robert G. O'Meally (New York: Columbia University Press, 1998).

3. Maya Angelou, *Singin' and Swingin' and Gettin' Merry Like Christmas* (New York: Random House, 2009).

4. Amiri Baraka, *Black Music* (New York: Akaschic Books, 2009).

5. In *Giant Steps: Bebop and the Creators of Modern Jazz 1945–65* (Edinburgh: Canongate Books, 1999), Kenny Mathieson notes: "According to Mary Lou Williams, it was Monk who first began to wear a beret and horn rim glasses but it was Dizzy who turned them into Bebop's trademark image" (Mathieson 161).

6. The quoted language is taken from Scott Deveaux's analysis of the photo spread in *Life*. See Scott Deveaux, *The Birth of Bebop: A Social and Musical History* (Berkeley: University of California Press, 1997).

7. See Sherrie Tucker, *Swing Shift: "All-Girl" Bands of the 1940s* (Durham, NC: Duke University Press, 2000).

8. Tammy Kernodle, *Soul on Soul: The Life and Music of Mary Lou Willliams* (Boston: Northeastern University Press, 2004).

9. In *The Masters of Bebop* (New York: Da Capo Press, 2001), Ira Gitler briefly comments on Williams's role in bebop: "Mention must be made of Mary Lou Williams who, like Hawkins and Johnson, came from the previous era, but who not only encouraged the modern musicians but participated actively in the movement with such compositions as *Kool*, *In the Land of OO-bla-dee*, *Knowledge*, and for Benny Goodman, *Lonely Moments*" (277).

10. Dave Gelly, *Being Prez: The Life and Music of Lester Young* (New York: Oxford University Press, 2007).

11. In *The Swing Era: The Development of Jazz, 1930–1945* (Oxford: Oxford University Press, 1989), Gunther Schuller states: "On 'D.B. Blues' (short for detention barrack) his tone is a little harder and narrower than before . . . with an ironic edge."

12. I am referring to Sherrie Tucker's claim that black women's fiction is a "site in which Black women have long written with authority." See Sherrie Tucker, "Where the Blues and the Truth Lay Hiding: Rememory of Jazz in Black Women's Fiction," *Frontiers: A Journal of Women Studies* 13, no. 2 (1993): 26–44.

2. MUSICAL SIGNIFYIN(G): A THEORY OF CRY AND RESPONSE IN GAYL JONES'S *CORREGIDORA*

1. See Janice Harris, "Gayl Jones' *Corregidora*." *Frontiers: A Journal of Women Studies* 5, no. 3 (Autumn 1980): 1–5; Claudia Tate, "Corregidora: Ursa's Blues Medley," *Black American Literature Forum* 13, no. 4 (Winter 1979): 139–41; Donia Allen, "The Role of the Blues in Gayl Jones' *Corregidora*," *Callaloo* 25, no. 1, Jazz Poetics: A Special Issue (Winter 2002): 257–73.

2. Gayl Jones, *Liberating Voices: Oral Tradition in African American Literature* (New York: Penguin, 1992).

3. Žižek goes on to cite a scene from Alfred Hitchcock to describe the voice and the gaze as "objects" rather than subjects. One of the heroines approaches a peculiar house, and from a spectator's point of view, the house seems to be staring back at her. In this scene, "the crucial point, of course, is that this gaze should not be subjectivized: it's not simply that 'there is somebody in the house,' we are, rather, dealing with a kind of empty, a priori gaze that cannot be pinpointed as determinate reality—she 'cannot see it all,' she is looking at a blind spot, and the object returns the gaze from this blind spot" (90).

3. THE JAZZ MOMENT: (RE)ENVISIONING RALPH ELLISON'S *INVISIBLE MAN* IN TONI MORRISON'S *THE BLUEST EYE*

1. See Albert Murray, "The Function of the Heroic Image," lecture, Wesleyan University, May 17, 1985, in *The Jazz Cadence of American Culture*, ed. Robert O'Meally (New York: Columbia University Press, 1998).

2. As I explain in the introduction, cry-and-response is a musical trope that carries with it a "telling effect" and can be read throughout the ritualized dialogue found in African American literature.

3. See Adam Gussow, *Seems Like Murder Here: Southern Violence and the Blues Tradition* (Chicago: University of Chicago Press, 2002), for a thorough discussion of the various blues weapons.

4. This analysis is informed by discussion of the Trueblood scene in Houston Baker, *Blues, Ideology and African American Literature: A Vernacular Theory* (Chicago: University of Chicago Press, 1984) and Carol Boyce Davies, *Black Women, Writing, and Identity: Migrations of the Subject* (New York: Routledge, 1994).

5. Here, I am not claiming that the jazz figure is morally irresponsible but that, in this particular case, Cholly refuses to acknowledge responsibility. As the text implies, although he is punished by the community and the law, he repeats his offense.

4. WILD WOMEN DON'T HAVE THE BLUES: IMPROVISING WOMEN IN TONI MORRISON'S *JAZZ* AND ANN PETRY'S *THE STREET*

1. According to Freddy Washington, a writer for the *New York Amsterdam News*, "Except for those who sang blues called spirituals in church, blues-singing women were once called 'wild women'" ("Torrie Sings about 'Wild Women,' Blues and Tradition," (8).

2. See Maria Cristina Nisco, "Dark Histories, Bright Revisions: Writing the Black Female Body," *Nebula* 3, no. 1 (April 2006): 65–72.

3. "Karintha" is the second track on Marion Brown, *Geechee Recollections*.

4. See Partha Miller, "Reflections on the Construction of Beauty," in *Cultural Encounters: Representing Otherness*, ed. Elizabeth Hallam (London and New York: Routledge, 2000).

5. In my discussion of jazz as both sound and sentiment, I am alluding to what Nathaniel Mackey describes as the music's telling inarticulacies. See Nathaniel Mackey, "Sound and Sentiment, Sound and Symbol," in *Discrepant Engagement: Dissonance, Cross-Culturality, and Experimental Writing*, 252–53.

5. JAZZ AND THE CARIBBEAN: THE FEMINIST JAZZ LENS IN EDWIDGE DANTICAT'S *BREATH, EYES, MEMORY*

1. In "Jazz: America's Classical Music," William Taylor notes, "Americans of African descent, in producing music which expressed themselves, not only developed a new musical vocabulary, they created a *classical* music—an authentic *American* music which articulated uniquely American feelings and thoughts, which eventually came to transcend ethnic boundaries" (21).

2. Transculturation, defined as cultural change induced by the introduction of elements of a foreign culture, is a term coined by sociologist Fernando Ortiz in *Cuban Counterpoint* (Durham, NC: Duke University Press, 1995). I use it here to describe the process by which the introduction of jazz induces a cultural change in traditions as evidenced through the main protagonist, Sophie Caco.

3. According to Dayan, many Erzulies exist, and they are regarded either as members of the same family or as different manifestations of the same deity. Depending on region, ritual, hounfort (temple surround), or even individual servitor, Erzulie's attributes and expressions vary. She has many names: Grande Erzulie, Erzulie Taureau, Erzulie Freda, Erzulie-gd-rouge, Erzulie Mapian, Erzulie-dos-bas, Erzulie Zandor, Erzulie-severine-belle-femme, Erzulie Dantor, Erzulie-coeur-noir, Erzulie-kokobe (Erzulie the shriveled), Erzulie-batala. Haitian orthography is varied, and the phonetic variants numerous. I use *Erzulie* as a general label: she has varying attributes in the novel.

4. See Harold Courlander, "Musical Instruments of Haiti," *Musical Quarterly* 27 (1941): 371–83.

5. See Claudine Michel and Patrick Bellgarde-Smith, eds., *Voudou in Haitian Life and Culture: Invisible Powers* (New York: Palgrave Macmillan, 2006).

6. See Joan Dayan, *Haiti, History, and the Gods* (Berkeley: University of California Press, 1995); and Maya Deren, *Divine Horsemen: The Living Gods of Haiti* (New Paltz, NY: McPherson, 1983).

6. *THE FISHER KING* AND THE WOMEN OF JAZZ

1. See Caroline Rosenthal's extensive chapter on *The Fisher King* in *New York and Toronto Novels after Postmodernism: Explorations of the Urban* (Rochester, NY: Camden House, 2011).

2. Marshall is not the only woman writer to appropriate jazz discourse. See Tucker, "Where the Blues and the Truth Lay Hiding," and Griffin, "It Takes Two People."

3. John Lowney, in "'A New Kind of Music': Jazz Improvisation and the Diasporic Dissonance of Paule Marshall's *The Fisher King*" (*MELUS* 40, no. 1 [2015]), posits Hattie Carmichael as a "co-protagonist."

4. For the politics of respectability, see Higginbotham, *Righteous Discontent*; and Candice Jenkins, *Private Lives, Proper Relations: Regulating Black Intimacy* (Minneapolis: University of Minnesota Press, 2007).

CONCLUSION: TOWARD A WOMANIST JAZZ LENS: GENDER AND JAZZ IN POETRY AND DANCE

1. See Alice Walker, *In Search of Our Mothers' Gardens: Womanist Prose*, 1st ed. (San Diego: Harcourt Brace Jovanovich, 1983)

2. I borrow the scene nomenclature from Wriggle, "The Mother of All Albums."

BIBLIOGRAPHY

Aiken, George. *Uncle Tom's Cabin.* New York: Garland, 1994.

Allen, Donia. "The Role of the Blues in Gayl Jones' *Corregidora.*" *Callaloo* 25, no. 1, Jazz Poetics: A Special Issue (Winter 2002): 257–73.

Angelou, Maya. "The Reunion." In *The Rough Road Home: Stories by North Carolina Authors,* ed. Robert Gingher. Chapel Hill: University of North Carolina Press, 1992.

Angelou, Maya. *Singin' and Swingin' and Gettin' Merry Like Christmas.* New York: Random House, 2009.

Baker, Houston A. *Blues Ideology, and Afro-American Literature: A Vernacular Theory.* Chicago: University of Chicago Press, 1984.

Baker, Houston A. "To Move without Moving: An Analysis of Creativity and Commerce in Ralph Ellison's Trueblood Episode." *PMLA* 98, no. 5 (1983): 828–45.

Baldwin, James. "Sonny's Blues." *Going to Meet the Man.* New York: Vintage, 1995.

Baraka, Amiri (LeRoi Jones). *Black Music.* New York: Akaschic Books, 2009.

Baraka, Amiri (LeRoi Jones). "The 'Blues Aesthetic' and the 'Black Aesthetick': Aesthetics as the Continuing Political History of a Culture." *Black Music Research Journal* 11, no. 2 (Autumn 1991): 101–9.

Baraka, Amiri (LeRoi Jones). *Blues People.* New York: William Morrow, 1963.

Baraka, Amiri (LeRoi Jones). *Dutchman and the Slave.* New York: Morrow, 1964.

Baraka, Amiri (LeRoi Jones). *The Leroi Jones/Amiri Baraka Reader.* New York: Thunder's Mouth Press, 2000.

Bechet, Sidney. *Treat It Gentle: An Autobiography.* Cambridge, MA: Da Capo Press, 2002.

Bell, Bernard. *The Afro-American Novel and Its Tradition.* Amherst: University of Massachusetts Press, 1987.

Berliner, Paul. *Thinking in Jazz: The Infinite Art of Improvisation.* Chicago: University of Chicago Press, 1994.

Bolden, Tony, and Jayne Cortez. "All the Birds Sing Bass: The Revolutionary Blues of Jayne Cortez." *African American Review* 35, no. 1 (2001): 61–71.

Boyce-Davies, Carole. *Black Women, Writing, and Identity: Migrations of the Subject.* London: Routledge, 1994.

Breton, Marcela, ed. *Hot and Cool Jazz Short Stories.* New York: Plume, 1980.

Brown, Caroline. "Golden Gray and the Talking Book: Identity as a Site of Artful Construction in Toni Morrison's *Jazz*." *African American Review* 36, no. 4 (Winter 2002): 629–42.

Burke, Kenneth. "Literature as Equipment for Living." In *The Critical Tradition: Classic Texts and Contemporary Trends*, ed. David H. Richter. Boston: Bedford/ St. Martin's, 1998.

Carby, Hazel. "It Jus Be's Dat Way Sometime: The Sexual Politics of Women's Blues." In *The Jazz Cadence of American Culture*, ed. Robert G. O'Meally. New York: Columbia University Press, 1998.

Carnig, Jennifer. "All That Jazz Could Be Heard in All Corners of Our World." *University of Chicago Chronicle* 25, no. 16 (May 11, 2006).

Chancy, Myriam J. A. *Framing Silence: Revolutionary Novels by Haitian Women*. New Brunswick, NJ: Rutgers University Press, 1997.

Chenard, Marc. "Instinct and Design: The Dialectics of Improvisational Music." Lecture. Guelph International Jazz Festival and Colloquium. University of Guelph, Ontario, 2000.

Collins, Patricia Hill. *Black Feminist Thought: Knowledge, Consciousness, and the Politics of Empowerment*. Boston: Unwin Hyman, 1990.

Courlander, Harold. "Musical Instruments of Haiti." *Musical Quarterly* XXVII (1941): 371–83.

Crouch, Stanley. "Blues to Be Constitutional: A Long Look at the Wild Wherefores of Our Democratic Lives as Symbolized in the Making of Rhythm and Tune." In *The Jazz Cadence of American Culture*, ed. Robert G. O'Meally. New York: Columbia University Press, 1998.

Danticat, Edwidge. *Breath, Eyes, Memory*. New York: Vintage Books, 1998.

Davis, Angela. *Blues Legacies and Black Feminism: Gertrude "Ma" Rainey, Bessie Smith, and Billie Holiday*. New York: Pantheon Books, 1998.

Dayan, Joan. *Haiti, History, and the Gods*. Berkeley: University of California Press, 1995.

DeFrantz, Thomas. "The Black Beat Made Visible: Hip Hop Dance and Body Power." In *Of the Presence of the Body: Essays on Dance and Performance Theory*, ed. André Lepecki. Middletown, CT: Wesleyan University Press, 2004.

Deren, Maya. *Divine Horsemen: The Living Gods of Haiti*. New Paltz, NY: McPherson, 1983.

Desmangles, Leslie G. *The Faces of the Gods: Vodou and Roman Catholicism in Haiti*. Chapel Hill: University of North Carolina Press, 1992.

Deveaux, Scott. *The Birth of Bebop: A Social and Musical History*. Berkeley: University of California Press, 1997.

Doane, Janice, and Devon Hodges. *Telling Incest: Narratives of Dangerous Remembering from Stein to Sapphire*. Ann Arbor: University of Michigan Press, 2001.

Edwards, Brent, Farah Griffin, and Robert G. O'Meally, eds. *Uptown Conversations: The New Jazz Studies*. New York: Columbia University Press, 2004.

Ellison, Ralph. *Invisible Man*. New York: Vintage Books, 1952.

Ellison, Ralph, and Robert G. O'Meally. *Living with Music: Ralph Ellison's Jazz Writings*. New York: Modern Library, 2001.

Ellison, Ralph. *Shadow and Act*. New York: Random House, 1953.

Floyd, Samuel A., Jr. *The Power of Black Music: Interpreting Its History from Africa to the United States*. New York: Oxford University Press, 1995.

Fox, Robert Elliot. "Diasporacentrism and Black Aural Texts." In *The African Diaspora: African Origins and New World Identities*, ed. Carole Boyce-Davies, Isidore Okpewho, and Ali Al'Amin Mazrui. Bloomington and Indianapolis: Indiana University Press, 2002.

Freud, Sigmund, and James Strachey. *Beyond the Pleasure Principle*. New York: Norton, 1989.

Gabbard, Krin, ed. *Jazz among the Discourses*. Durham, NC: Duke University Press, 1995.

Gelly, Dave. *Being Prez: The Life and Music of Lester Young*. New York: Oxford University Press, 2007.

Giddins, Gary. *Giant Steps: Bebop and the Creators of Modern Jazz, 1945–65*. New York: W. W. Norton, 2009.

Gioia, Ted. *The History of Jazz*. New York: Oxford University Press, 2011.

Gitler, Ira. *Masters of Bebop: A Listener's Guide*. New York: Da Capo Press, 2001.

Gordon, Linda. "Incest and Resistance: Patterns of Father-Daughter Incest, 1880–1930." *Social Problems* 33, no. 4 (April 1986): 253–67.

Grandt, Jurgen E. *Kinds of Blue: The Jazz Aesthetic in African American Narrative*. Columbus: Ohio State University Press, 2004.

Greenblatt, Stephen. "Improvisation and Power." In *Literature and Society*, ed. Edward Said. Baltimore: Johns Hopkins University Press, 1980.

Griffin, Farah J. "It Takes Two People to Confirm the Truth: The Jazz Fiction of Sherley Ann Williams and Toni Cade Bambara." In *Big Ears: Listening for Gender in Jazz Studies*, ed. Nichole T. Rustin and Sherrie Tucker. Durham, NC: Duke University Press, 2008.

Griffin, Farah J. "Ladies Sing Miles." In *Miles Davis and American Culture*, ed. Gerald Early. St. Louis: Missouri Historical Society Press, 2001.

Griffin, Farah J. *"Who Set You Flowin'?": The African-American Migration Narrative*. New York: Oxford University Press, 1995.

Gussow, Adam. *Seems Like Murder Here: Southern Violence and the Blues Tradition*. Chicago: University of Chicago Press, 2002.

Hall, Stuart. "Cultural Identity and Diaspora." In Identity: *Community, Culture, Difference*, ed. Jonathan Rutherford. London: Lawrence and Wishart, 1990.

Harper, Michael. "An Interview with Gayl Jones." In *Chant of Saints: A Gathering of Afro-American Literature, Art, and Scholarship*, ed. Michael S. Harper and Robert B. Stepto. Urbana: University of Illinois Press, 1979.

Harris, Janice. "Gayl Jones' *Corregidora*." *Frontiers: A Journal of Women Studies* 5, no. 3 (Autumn 1980): 1–5.

Harris, Wilson. *The Womb of Space: The Cross-cultural Imagination*. Westport, CT: Greenwood Press, 1983.

Hawkins, Alfonso. *The Jazz Trope: A Theory of African American Literary and Vernacular Culture*. Lanham, MD: Scarecrow Press, 2008.

Heller, Dana. "Anatomies of Rape." *American Literary History* 16, no. 2 (2004): 329–49.

Herman, Judith. *Father-Daughter Incest*. Cambridge, MA: Harvard University Press, 1981.

Higginbotham, Evelyn Brooks. *Righteous Discontent: The Women's Movement in the Black Baptist Church, 1880–1920*. Cambridge, MA: Harvard University Press, 1993.

hooks, bell. *Talking Back: Thinking Feminist, Thinking Black*. Boston: South End Press, 1989.

Horovitz, Deborah. *Literary Trauma: Sadism, Memory, and Sexual Violence in American Women's Fiction*. Albany: State University of New York Press, 2000.

Imorou, Nassourou. "To Walk or to Fly? The Legend of the Flying Africans in Toni Morrison's Song of Solomon and Paule Marshall's Praisesong for the Widow." *Research on Humanities and Social Sciences* 7, no. 2 (2017): 48–54.

James, Willis Laurence. *Stars in De Elements: A Study of Negro Folk Music*. Durham, NC: Duke University Press, 1995.

Jenkins, Candice. *Private Lives, Proper Relations: Regulating Black Intimacy*. Minneapolis: University of Minnesota Press, 2007.

Jones, Gayl. *Corregidora*. New York: Random House, 1975.

Jones, Gayl. *Eva's Man*. Boston: Beacon Press, 1976.

Jones, Gayl. *Liberating Voices: Oral Tradition in African American Literature*. New York: Penguin, 1992.

Kebede, Ashenafi. *Roots of Black Music*. Englewood Cliffs, NJ: Prentice-Hall, 1982.

Kernodle, Tammy. *Soul on Soul: The Life and Music of Mary Lou Willliams*. Boston: Northeastern University Press, 2004.

Lacan, Jacques. *The Four Fundamental Concepts of Psycho-Analysis*. New York: W. W. Norton, 1981.

Lewis, Leslie. *Telling Narratives: Secrets in African American Literature*. Urbana: University of Illinois Press, 2007.

Litweiler, John. *The Freedom Principle: Jazz after 1958*. New York: W. Morrow, 1984.

Lowney, John. "'A New Kind of Music': Jazz Improvisation and the Diasporic Dissonance of Paule Marshall's *The Fisher King*." *MELUS* 40, no. 1 (2015): 99–123.

Mackey, Nathaniel. "Sound and Sentiment, Sound and Symbol." In *Discrepant Engagement: Dissonance, Cross-Culturality, and Experimental Writing*. Tuscaloosa: University of Alabama Press, 1993.

Marcos, Ana Maria Fraile. "Lady Sings the Blues: Gayl Jones' *Corregidora*." In *Literature and Music*, ed. Michael J. Meyer. New York: Rodopi, 2002.

Marshall, Paule. *The Fisher King*. New York: Scribner, 2000.

Mathieson, Kenny. *Giant Steps: Bebop and the Creators of Modern Jazz, 1945–65*. Edinburgh: Canongate Books, 1999.

Meigs, Anna, and Kathleen Barlow. "Beyond the Taboo: Imagining Incest." *American Anthropologist* 104, no. 1 (2002): 38–49.

Michel, Claudine. "Voudou in Haiti: Way of Life and Mode of Survival." In *Voudou in Haitian Life and Culture: Invisible Powers*, ed. Claudine Michel and Patrick Bellgarde-Smith. New York: Palgrave Macmillan, 2006.

Miller, Partha. "Reflections on the Construction of Beauty." In *Cultural Encounters: Representing Otherness*, ed. Elizabeth Hallam. London and New York: Routledge, 2000.

Mitchell, Angelyn. *The Freedom to Remember: Narrative, Slavery, and Gender in Contemporary Black Women's Fiction*. New Brunswick, NJ: Rutgers University Press, 2002.

Morrison, Toni. *The Bluest Eye*. New York: Plume Book: [1970] 2005.

Morrison, Toni. *Jazz*. New York: Knopf, 1992.

Murray, Albert. *The Blue Devils of Nada: A Contemporary Approach to Aesthetic Statement*. New York: Vintage Books, 1997.

Murray, Albert. "The Function of the Heroic Image." Lecture. Wesleyan University, May 17, 1985. In *The Jazz Cadence of American Culture*, ed. Robert O'Meally. New York: Columbia University Press, 1998.

Murray, Albert. *The Hero and the Blues*. New York: Random House, 1973.

Murray, Albert. "Improvisation and the Creative Process." In *Stirrings of Culture*, ed. Robert J. Sardello and Gail Thomas. Dallas: Dallas Institute Publications, 1986.

Murray, Albert. *Stomping the Blues*. New York: Da Capo Press, 1989.

Murray, Albert. *Train Whistle Guitar*. New York: Random House, 1974.

Nisco, Maria Christina. "Dark Histories, Bright Revisions: Writing the Black Female Body." *Nebula* 3, no. 1 (April 2006): 65–72.

O'Laughlin, Jim. "Articulating Uncle Tom's Cabin." *New Literary History* 31, no. 3 (Summer 2000).

O'Meally, Robert, ed. *The Jazz Cadence of American Culture*. New York: Columbia University Press, 2004.

Ortiz, Fernando. *Cuban Counterpoint: Tobacco and Sugar*. Durham, NC: Duke University Press, 1995.

Peterson, Carla. "Capitalism, Black (Under) Development, and the Production of the African-American Novel in the 1850s." *American Literary History* 4, no. 4 (Winter 1992): 559–83.

Petry, Ann. *The Street*. New York: Houghton Mifflin, 1946.

Pettis, Joyce. "She Sung Back in Return": Literary (Re)vision and Transformation in Gayl Jones's *Corregidora*." *College English* 52, no. 7 (November 1990): 787–99.

Pierce, Yolanda. "Restless Spirits: Syncretic Religion in Edwidge Danticat's *Breath, Eyes, Memory*." *Journal of Pan African Studies* 3, no. 5 (2010): 68–77.

Porter, Eric. *What Is This Thing Called Jazz? African American Musicians as Artists, Critics, and Activists*. Berkeley: University of California Press, 2002.

Powell, Richard. *The Blues Aesthetic: Black Culture and Modernism*. Washington, DC: Washington Project for the Arts, 1989.

Rosenthal, Caroline. *New York and Toronto Novels after Postmodernism: Explorations of the Urban*. Rochester, NY: Camden House, 2011.

Rustin, Nicole, and Sherrie Tucker, eds. *Big Ears: Searching for Gender in Jazz Studies*. Durham, NC: Duke University Press, 2008.

Schuller, Gunther. *The Swing Era: The Development of Jazz, 1930–1945*. Oxford: Oxford University Press, 1989.

Scott, William. "Material Resistance and the Agency of the Body in Ann Petry's *The Street*." *American Literature* 78, no. 1 (2006): 89–116.

Sielke, Sabine. *Reading Rape: The Rhetoric of Sexual Violence in American Literature and Culture, 1790–1990*. Princeton, NJ: Princeton University Press, 2002.

Smith, Cynthia. "Gayl Jones." In *African American Writers*, ed. Lea Brechler and A. Walton Litz. New York: Charles Scribner's Sons, 1991.

Soler, Colette. "The Subject and the Other." In *Reading Seminar XI: Lacan's Four Fundamental Concepts of Psychoanalysis*, ed. Richard Feldstein, Bruce Fink, and Maire Jaanus. Albany: State University of New York Press, 1995.

Southern, Eileen. *The Music of Black Americans: A History*. New York: W. W. Norton, 1971.

Spillers, Hortense. *Black, White, and in Color: Essays on American Literature and Culture*. Chicago: University of Chicago Press, 2003.

Stearns, Marshall W. *The Story of Jazz*. New York: Oxford University Press, 1956.

Stepto, Robert. *From Behind the Veil: A Study of African American Narrative*. Urbana: University of Illinois Press, 1979.

Stowe, Harriet Beecher. *Uncle Tom's Cabin*. London: J. Cassell, 1852.

Szwed, John. *Jazz 101: A Complete Guide to Learning and Loving Jazz*. New York: Hyperion Press, 2000.

Tate, Claudia. "*Corregidora*: Ursa's Blues Medley." *Black American Literature Forum* 13, no. 4 (1970): 139–41.

Taylor, William "Billy." "Jazz: America's Classical Music." In *Black Perspective in Music* 14, no. 1, Special Issue: Black American Music Symposium 1985 (Winter 1986): 21–25.

Toomer, Jean. *Cane*. New York: University Place Press, 1967.

Tracy, Steven. "The Blues Novel." In *The Cambridge Companion to the African American Novel*, ed. Maryemma Graham. New York: Cambridge University Press, 2004.

Tucker, Mark, ed. *The Duke Ellington Reader*. New York: Oxford University Press, 1993.

Tucker, Sherrie. *Swing Shift: "All-Girl" Bands of the 1940s*. Durham, NC: Duke University Press, 2000.

Tucker, Sherrie. "Where the Blues and the Truth Lay Hiding: Rememory of Jazz in Black Women's Fiction." *Frontiers: A Journal of Women Studies* 13, no. 2 (1993): 26–44.

Urban, Greg. "Ritual Wailing in Amerindian Brazil." *American Anthropologist*, New Series 90, no. 2 (June 1988): 385–400.

Vogel, Shane. *Stolen Time: Black Fad Performance and the Calypso Craze*. Chicago: University of Chicago Press, 2018.

Walker, Alice. *In Search of Our Mothers' Gardens: Womanist Prose*. San Diego: Harcourt Brace Jovanovich, 1984.

Wall, Cheryl. *Worrying the Line: Black Women Writers, Lineage, and Literary Tradition*. Chapel Hill: University of North Carolina Press, 2005.

Wallace, Kimberly, ed. *Skin Deep, Spirit Strong: The Black Female Body in American Culture*. Ann Arbor: University of Michigan Press, 2002.

Washington, Freddy. "'Torrie Sings about 'Wild Women,' Blues and Tradition." *New York Amsterdam News*, April 23, 1988, 26.

Williams, Jennifer. "Jean Toomer's *Cane* and the Erotics of Mourning." *Southern Literary Journal* 40, no. 2 (Spring 2008): 87–101.

Wilson, Harriet. *Our Nig, or, Sketches from the Life of a Free Black*. Boston: Geo. C. Rand & Avery, 1859.

Wintz, Cary D. and Paul Finkelman, eds. *Encyclopedia of the Harlem Renaissance*. New York: Routledge, 2004.

Wriggle, John. "The Mother of All Albums." In *Duke Ellington Studies*, ed. John Howland. New York: Cambridge University Press, 2017.

Wright, Richard "Foreword." In Paul Oliver, *Blues Fell This Morning: The Meaning of the Blues*. Toronto: Macmillan, 1960.

Žižek, Slavoj. "'I Hear You with My Eyes'; or, The Invisible Master." In *Gaze and Voice as Love Objects*, ed. Renata Salecl and Slavoj Žižek, 90–126. Durham, NC: Duke University Press, 1996.

INDEX

African diaspora literature, 91, 126;
  women writers, 8
agency, 11, 111; in *Corregidora*, 45;
  through improvisation, 11, 17, 71;
  Wild Women and, 71, 74
Aiken, George, 72–73
Allen, Donia, 28
Angelou, Maya, 8, 16–27
Armstrong, Louis, 49, 52, 70
Autobiography of an Ex-Colored Man
  (Johnson), 7

Baartman, Saartjie, 72, 73
Baldwin, James, 8, 123, 124
Bambara, Toni Cade, 9
Baraka, Amiri, 7–9, 18–19, 70–71, 74, 119
Beat Generation, 7
bebop, 6, 8, 10, 16, 18, 95–96, 123, 127,
  134n5, 134n9; birth of, 19–20; coded
  language of, 18–19; masculinity of,
  19; origin of word, 77; transport, 19
Bechet, Sidney, 70
*Being Prez: The Life and Music of Lester
  Young* (Gelly), 21
Berliner, Paul, 47, 114
"Beyond the Pleasure Principle" (Freud),
  32–33
*Big Ears: Listening for Gender in Jazz
  Studies*, 8–9
"Black and Blue" (Armstrong), 49, 70
Black family, dissolution of, 65–66
Black Is Beautiful movement, 65
Black Music (Baraka), 18

Black power, 10
Black women: abuse of, 130–32; commodification of, 41, 45, 55, 76; family and, 65–66; historical representation of, 87; historical trauma,
  31; identity, 71, 86–87; policing the
  bodies of, 6; politics of respectability, 6, 133n2; resistance, 27, 71;
  sexuality of, 72–73, 87; subjectivity,
  8, 87, 128–32
Blue Note, the, 92
blues, 4, 79, 105; Black power and, 10;
  break, 28; classic blues period/
  tradition, 5, 10–11; discourse, 10–11;
  empowerment through, 70; formal
  devices of, 28, 36; literature, 10,
  28–30; lyrics, 60; women's role in,
  10, 68–71, 74
Blues Fell This Morning (Oliver), 47
Blues for Rampart Street (Cox), 68
Blues Legacies and Black Feminism
  (Davis), 68–69
"Blues to Be Constitutional" (Crouch),
  44
Bluest Eye, The (Morrison), 47–66;
  Aunt Jimmy, 57–58, 60; blues in,
  52–53, 57, 61; break in, 62–63; Cholly
  Breedlove, 48–49, 52–54, 56–66,
  95–96, 135n5; Cholly's father, 60;
  Cholly's mother, 57; Claudia Mac-
  Teer, 49, 56; cry-and-response in,
  53–54, 65; Darlene, 58–60; death
  in, 57–58, 60; dialogue in, 65;

125; improvisation in, 110, 112, 114–17, 119, 122–25; jacket copy, 110; jazz in, 110–12, 116, 118–22, 124–25; jazz moment in, 118–19, 122–23; the Maconettes, 117, 120; memorial concert, 120–22; Miss Grandiflora, 115–16; narration, 111, 120, 122, 124–25; oral tradition in, 112, 119, 125; power struggles in, 117–18; sexuality in, 117–18; SS *Nerissa*, 113; title, 110; Ulene Payne, 112–14, 116, 122; Wild Women in, 112, 117

Four Fundamental Concepts, The (Lacan), 37

Fox, Robert, 91, 92

freedom, attainment of, 10; in *The Bluest Eye*, 57–59, 61–62; in *Breath, Eyes, Memory*, 101–2, 108; in *Corregidora*, 28–29, 45–46, 52; in *The Fisher King*, 115; in *Invisible Man*, 51–52; jazz and, 66; Wild Woman and, 74

Freud, Sigmund, 32–33, 37

Freytag's narrative pyramid, 120

Gabbard, Krin, 53

Geechee Recollections (Brown), 136n3

Gelly, Dave, 21

Gillespie, Dizzy, 18–20, 134n5

Gioia, Ted, 3–4

Gitler, Ira, 134n9

Goodman, Benny, 19

Grandt, Jurgen, 7, 70

Great Migration, 93, 115

Griffin, Farah Jasmine, 7–10, 96

Gross, Terry, 85–86

Haiti: call-and-response, 107–8; cultural traditions, 89–91; jazz music and, 90; oral tradition, 107; voodoo and, 90–91, 94

Harlem, 93

Harlem Renaissance, 79

Hawkins, Coleman, 68

Higginbotham, Evelyn Brooks, 5–6

History of Jazz, The (Gioia), 3–4

Hitchcock, Alfred, 135n3

hooks, bell, 45

Hughes, Langston, 7, 70, 77

Hurston, Zora Neale, 90

hysterical subject, 33

"'I Hear You with My Eyes'; or, The Invisible Master" (Žižek), 37

"If a Drum Is a Woman" (Cortez), 6–7, 129–32; improvisational resistance in, 129–30; narrative structure of, 130; repetition in, 131–32; rhetorical questions in, 7, 130; violence in, 129–30

Imorou, Nassourou, 129

improvisation, 16, 27, 47, 71, 85–86, 127–28; agency through, 17, 71; in *The Bluest Eye*, 54, 57, 60–62, 64, 95–96; in *Breath, Eyes, Memory*, 95, 97–98; in *Corregidora*, 29, 31–32, 35, 44; definition of, 66; in *A Drum Is a Woman*, 129; in *The Fisher King*, 110, 112, 114–19, 122–25; in "If a Drum Is a Woman," 129–30; in *Invisible Man*, 49, 50, 52, 54; in *Jazz*, 67; linguistic signifiers, 47; moment of, 8, 10, 15, 27, 47, 54, 87, 95–98, 112, 118–19, 122–23; process of, 47; resistance through, 71, 126; in "The Reunion," 24, 27; in *The Street*, 77, 85; subjectivity through, 17; Wild Women and, 71

"Improvisation and the Creative Process" (Murray), 21

In Search of Our Mothers' Gardens: Womanist Prose (Walker), 126–27

"In Walked Bud," 18

intercultural identity, 8

intimate violence, 7, 15

Invisible Man (Ellison), 47, 83; blues in, 60–61, 64–66; cry-and-response in, 49–51; freedom in, 51–52; improvisation in, 49, 50, 52, 54; incest in, 47–49, 54–55, 56, 60–61, 63–65; Invisible Man, 24, 50–52, 64, 70; jazz in, 50–52; Kate, 55, 60–61; Matty Lou, 49, 54–56, 61, 63–64; Mr. Norton, 55; narrative, 49, 52, 55–56; old woman in, 50–51; prologue, 49; sermon in, 50; shame in, 49; Trueblood, 48–49, 54–56, 60–61, 63–66; Wild Woman, 49, 52

Jackson, Travis, 90
James, Willis, 34
jazz: 1970s and 1980s, 7; African diaspora women's writing and, 3–15; birth of/origins, 4–5, 19, 79, 91–92, 136n1; the "break," 11, 21–22, 28, 31, 35, 62–63, 119–21; call-and-response, 34–36, 42, 90, 92, 103, 107–9, 112, 123, 127; cry-and-response, 8, 10–11, 15, 28–46, 49–51, 53–54, 65, 87–88, 96, 126, 135n2; cultural influence, 7, 15; freedom and, 66; group dynamics, 125; Haitian culture and, 90; improvisation, 8, 10, 15–17, 24, 27, 29, 31–32, 35, 44, 47, 49–50, 52, 54, 57, 60–62, 64, 66–67, 71, 77, 85–87, 95–98, 110, 112, 114–19, 122–30; influence on Black women's fiction, 7; literary discourse, 7–8; literature, 8–10, 27, 29–30, 74, 85, 123, 127; literature, Caribbean American, 10, 89–109; literature, definition of, 9–10; literature, feminist, 9–10, 15; literature, gendered reading of, 8; literature, resistance through, 27; literature, "worrying the line," 16; malleability, 87; moment, 11, 15, 21–22, 24, 28, 44, 47–67, 95, 118–19, 123, 133n8; musical social organization of,

124–25; repetition, 31, 35, 42, 131–32; resistance through, 65–66; revision, 31–32; rhythm structure, 7, 30; role of women in, 3, 5–7, 10–12, 15–27, 68, 70–71, 74, 88, 111, 123, 127; slavery and, 90; violence in, 64, 77, 79, 85–86, 97
Jazz (Morrison), 8, 67, 70–71, 79; Alice Manfred, 81–83, 86, 97; cry in, 87–88; Dorcas Manfred, 67, 68, 80–81, 84–86; Felice, 80; Golden Grey, 81; Hunters Hunter, 81; Jazz, 79; jazz moment of improvisation, 67, 85–86; jazz music in, 68, 80–81, 83–84; Joe Trace, 67–68, 80, 82–84, 86; narration, 79, 81–82; opening lines, 80; Rose Dear, 82; violence in, 81, 83–86; Violet, 67–68, 80–85, 96; Wild, 67, 68, 80–82, 84; Wild Women in, 67–68, 70, 79–82, 84–85
Jazz 101 (Szwed), 30
"Jazz: America's Classical Music" (Taylor), 136n1
Jazz Among the Discourse (Gabbard), 53
jazz moment, 11, 15, 21, 47–66, 133n8; in *The Bluest Eye*, 48–49, 54, 57, 60, 64; in *Breath, Eyes, Memory*, 95; in *Corregidora*, 28, 44; in *The Fisher King*, 118–19, 123; in *Invisible Man*, 49; in *Jazz*, 67; in "The Reunion," 22, 24
Jim Crow laws, 121
Johnson, J. J., 20
Johnson, James Weldon, 7
Johnson, Lyndon, 65
Jones, Gayl, 8, 10, 28–46, 50

"Karintha" (Brown), 75, 136n3
Kebede, Ashenafi, 34
Kernodle, Tammy, 20
Kerouac, Jack, 7
Ku Klux Klan, 121

"Sonny's Blues" (Baldwin), 123–24
*Soul on Soul: The Life and Music of
    Mary Lou Williams* (Kernodle), 20
spirituals, 93–95, 127
Stepto, Robert B., 123
Stowe, Harriet Beecher, 71–73
Street, The (Petry), 7, 67, 70–71, 75–76;
    abuse in, 76; Beau Beau Weavil, 78;
    Beau Ella Thornhill, 78–79; blues
    in, 78; Boots Smith, 70, 75–78, 86;
    Bub, 75–76, 78; Granny, 75; impro-
    visation in, 77; jazz in, 78; Junto, 76;
    Little Buddy, 78; Lutie Johnson, 70,
    75–79, 82, 86, 96; Mrs. Chandler,
    75–76; Mrs. Hedges, 76; murder in,
    77–79; narrator, 78; Papa Gumbo
    Willie Worthy, 78; sexuality in, 75–
    76; the Super, 76, 78; Vanderbilt
    Coleman, 78; Wild Women in, 70,
    75–77
"Subject and the Other, The" (Soler), 33
swing music, 18
Szwed, John, 30, 124

Tate, Claudia, 28
Taylor, William, 136n1
"Tell Martha Not to Moan" (Williams),
    9
*Thinking in Jazz: The Infinite Art of
    Improvisation* (Berliner), 47
Time magazine, 86
Toomer, Jean, 74
transculturation, 136n2
Treat It Gentle (Bechet), 70
Tucker, Sherrie, 7–10, 19, 134n12
Tyne, Margaret, 127–28

Uncle Tom's Cabin (Stowe), 71; Gump-
    tion Cute, 73; theater adaptation
    of, 72–73; Topsy, 72–73
Urban, Greg, 42, 43
US Steel Hour, 5, 128–29

Vogel, Shane, 129

wailing, ritual, 42–43
Walker, Alice, 126–27
Wall, Cheryl, 16, 23
Wallace, Kimberly, 71
Washington, Freddy, 136n1
"Where the Blues and the Truth Lay
    Hiding" (Tucker), 8
Wild Child, 72–73
Wild Woman, 7–8, 10–11, 15, 67–88,
    126–27, 136n1; armed, 67, 68, 74, 79–
    80, 85, 87; blues women, 68–71; in
    The Bluest Eye, 48; in *Breath, Eyes,
    Memory*, 96, 106; in *Corregidora*,
    28, 37–38, 46; definition of, 6, 11, 68,
    72; in *A Drum Is a Woman*, 6, 129;
    empowerment of, 70–71, 74; Erzulie
    as, 100; evolution of, 73–74; as a fig-
    ure of resistance, 6, 11; in *The Fisher
    King*, 112, 117; in *Invisible Man*, 49,
    52; in *Jazz*, 67–68, 70, 79–82, 84–86;
    jazz women, 70–71; stereotypes re-
    garding, 67–68, 72; in *The Street*, 70,
    75–77, 86
"Wild Women Don't Have the Blues"
    (Cox), 68, 69
Williams, Jennifer D., 74–75
Williams, Mary Lou, 16, 19–22, 134n5,
    134n9
Williams, Sherley Ann, 9
Wilson, Harriet, 73
Wilson, Lillian Carter, 19
womanism/womanist readings, 126–28,
    132
World War II, 5, 9
"worrying the line," 16
Wright, Richard, 8, 47

Young, Lester, 21

Žižek, Slavoj, 37, 135n3

ABOUT THE AUTHOR

Dr. Patricia G. Lespinasse is associate professor of African American and African diaspora literature in the Department of Africana Studies at Binghamton University, State University of New York. She teaches courses in blues/jazz literature, Caribbean literature, Africana studies, and race, gender, and American film.

9 781496 836021